This Was Football

This Was Football

by W. W. "Pudge" Heffelfinger

as told to
John McCallum

A. S. Barnes and Company · New York

Contents

Foreword

By Grantland Rice

As we look them over in the big corral
As the years march by—as they rise and fall—
Here's to big Pudge—my pick and my pal—
The greatest Roman of them all.

I witnessed my first football game in 1892, back in the sport's stone age when Pudge Heffelfinger was boyhood's idol and his feats of strength were even then legendary—when poets were moved to write lines like, "Linger, oh, linger, Heffelfinger!"

The granddaddy of the Old Blues was unquestionably the most amazing football player I have ever known.

Pudge was the only football player in history whose active playing career extended over a fifty-year span. Think of it—football! Fifty years! When he was forty-eight years old, for example, he returned to New Haven to tutor the Yale line and handled the varsity linemen so vigorously in scrimmage that they had to order the "old man" out of there before he wrecked the team.

When he was fifty-four, or thereabouts, Heffelfinger played fifty-eight minutes of an all-star charity game in Columbus between Minnesota and Ohio State graduates, most of them just out of college. Even a sprained shoulder couldn't force him off the field. The late Bo McMillin played with Pudge that afternoon and to his dying day attested that the old Yale immortal was the fastest man on the field.

"He was absolutely unbelievable," McMillin told me. "He came out of the line like a thunderbolt and he was fifty-four years old."

Heffelfinger played his last game in Minneapolis at the age of sixty-five in a pro charity benefit. To borrow a line from old Bill Shakespeare: "Cowards die many times before their death. The valiant never taste of death but once."

A few years ago I had Pudge as guest on a radio program of mine and he said, "Who ever said football was a rough game, Grant? I played it for almost fifty years. I know I was better at forty-five than I was at twenty. But I'll have to admit I'd slowed down a little when I was sixty-five. Not much—but a little. All I can say is that I started out at Yale in 1888 and would like just one more shot before I turn in my cleats."

Here was a man, pressing eighty at the time, and still wistful about getting back in there for a few more licks!

John McCallum, a pretty fair college athlete himself a decade ago, told me that he was never so amazed in all his life as when he interviewed Heffelfinger for the first time. Pudge was past eighty, but was still hard as a block of granite and weighed 240. The question of line play came up. Pudge knuckled down on the carpet, and John took to his heels for fear the old Eli would "take off" and push him through the wall. Pudge got up easily, and brushed his graying hair back from his ruddy face.

"Say," he snorted, "I'm getting kinda old, but I could go out on a field tomorrow and for three or four minutes

I could show you how we used to do it in the olden days. Why, I'd just give 'em this," and he clasped his hands together and swung both arms with a great pendulum sweep that would have bowled over any charging lineman.

When you looked at Pudge, you almost expected to see, in the background, the mystic figures of John L. Sullivan, Pop Anson, Snapper Garrison, Harry Vardon, Barney Oldfield and other unbelievables of the bygone sports era. Joe Williams once said that he had heard and read so much about Pudge that, until he actually met him, he was certain the old boy never existed. Surely, Heffelfinger was an incredible literary invention of some science fiction writer, very likely one of Gargantua's rowdy companions. Say, wasn't he the fellow who tore up the Princeton stadium by the roots and threw it halfway across the State of New Jersey? Didn't he send all the other Yales to the bench in one game and beat Harvard with one hand, 150-0? And how about the time he picked up a Pennsylvania fullback in the palm of his hand and squeezed the very life out of him? These are admittedly slight exaggerations, of course, but you get my point.

There never will be another Heffelfinger.

Ol' Pudge, Mr. Football. He was the greatest guard of all time, certainly a member of my all-time All-America . . . a fine old gentleman they have never stopped talking about in awed whispers under the elms at Yale.

In a football gathering, or near things related to the game, Pudge gave forth an aura of shining light, a special, ageless glory. He was the living symbol of the game, indestructible and forever young. Oldsters and youngsters alike worshipped him.

Not long before Pudge died he received a letter from a twelve-year-old boy. "Father tells me that you were the greatest football guard that ever played the game," the youth wrote. "Boy, that surely is going some. . . ." This many years after Pudge had left the field for good. Another letter arrived about the same time. "I have seen you play on the field many times," it said. "I have seen you with two of the opposition hanging on but still you used to plunge forward. You were indeed a One-Man Army. . . ." (Signed) Bernard M. Baruch.

It isn't generally known, but Pudge had much to do with founding the New York Touchdown Club. In October of 1933, he got together with Charley Pearson, John Heisman, Red Cagle, Alex Smith, and Bill Langford, Jr., son of the football rules-maker, at the old Downtown Athletic Club in Manhattan and discussed the possibility of forming an organization to aid intercollegiate football. The idea was to bring about a fraternity of those who had scored a touchdown in college—hence, The Touchdown Club. From that first meeting spawned what is today one of the most unique football groups in America, and its president, Henderson Van Surdam, the old football official, carries on in the Heffelfinger tradition.

When it came to telling the real story of football, I couldn't name a better person qualified to tell it—and Pudge's Boswell, John McCallum, did a wonderful job catching the old fellow's true flavor. Pudge had been around from the beginning, his mind was as clear as mountain air right up to the end, and nobody spun a tale better.

His recollections make a splendid book, one that definitely belongs in every sports fan's library. It takes you back to the misty canvas-jacketed era, brings roaring across the gridiron in all their glory the delightful likes of Pa Corbin, Snake Ames, Lonny Stagg, Gil Dobie, Hurry-Up Yost, Knute Rockne . . . George Gipp, Red Grange, Jim Thorpe, Bronko Nagurski . . . the Four Horsemen . . . Ernie Nevers . . . well, all of the immortals. No one told a funnier story than Pudge and this book has a million of them about exciting times.

This Was Football, by W. W. (Pudge) Heffelfinger as told to John McCallum, spans the glorious past and the ever-changing present with a bridge of wonderful memories.

So, here's to the memory of big Pudge . . . "my pick and my pal—The greatest Roman of them all."

Introduction

By Chet LaRoche
Chairman of the National Football Hall of Fame
and The National Football Foundation

Some of what will be said here is an exaggeration. There is no other way to get over a sense of what Pudge Heffelfinger was and believed in. For he, himself, was an exaggeration of most of the things a man likes to find in a man.

In any group—small or large, even up to banquet size —you "felt" Heff. If he didn't happen to be the most important man in the room, he was certainly the most compelling. Everyone in the room was aware he was there.

What I'm writing is only an introduction; there's just no way in these few pages, written to prepare the readers' mind for what is to come, of crowding so big a man into such a small space.

As I talked over this introduction with John McCallum, the author, and read an early draft of his manuscript, it was at a time when the newspapers were filled with news of the passing of Pudge Heffelfinger. They were also filled with dispatches from Dienbienphu—where the French were battling.

Into my office glided a muscular ex-athlete from Washington State, now a top-grade author of sports books. He came in to talk about Pudge's passing and his plans for finishing the book he'd started writing with Pudge about six months before. He spoke of Pudge reverently.

He knew what I thought of Pudge and Pudge had told him he'd like to have me write the introduction. I happened to play quarterback and played on the last Yale team Pudge helped coach—and being on the light side I guess Pudge wondered how I ever escaped alive in games against Harvard and Princeton.

Perhaps what is remembered about old football players is sentimental, slobbery stuff that only has meaning to a group of fanatics. At least that is what many professors think.

But I wonder if that is all there is to it. Why is it that every robust American lad tries his hand at the game? Why is it that without any compulsion or any inducement of any kind, Saturday after Saturday all fall, a great majority of the student body of every college in the country sits in the stands and cheers madly and feels elated or sad, according to the results? That's been going on for a long time. There must be something very elemental and satisfying and important to the nation that this is so.

Evidently there is something to be learned . . . from Heff and what happened at Dienbienphu. For the world watched Dienbienphu, as that distinguished columnist Henson Baldwin put it so well in the *New York Times*.

Whether France won or lost at Dienbienphu, they once more gave evidence to the fact that man and not the Hydrogen Bomb is still supreme on the battlefield. The will to fight . . . the fighting heart . . . indomitable, unbowed in the shadow of terrible odds is more than ever the essential foundation of victory in the age of weapons and mass destruction.

Man is still the master of the machine and the arbiter of all things. In a real sense some of the history of tomorrow was written by the bayonets of Colonel DeCastries and his stout soldiers.

In a real sense Heff for fifty long years, on and off the football field, gave a valiant exhibition—in fact, he was the embodiment of The Fighting Heart. Isn't that what Heff will always mean to us? Isn't that important? I think it is.

As long as there are men who will pay the price for their convictions, as long as there are men who put the spirit above the flesh, just that long will America be provided with the will to win this battle for the integrity and place of all men in the brotherhood that must come if our way of life is to survive. So, I'm happy to set down a few thoughts of ol' Mr. Football himself.

Right up to the day of his death, April 2, 1954, no one who knew the beloved gentleman, who had listened to him talk football, would have dreamed of referring to him as an "ex-football player." He never "retired."

Pudge Heffelfinger was eighty-six at the time of his passing. Unlike the other handful of great stars of all time, the Yale immortal had never stopped being a football player—even when he became a business man. He would have played in a game at eighty-six if anyone had given him the chance.

Age withered Pudge very little, nor did it stale the infinite variety of the stories he told about football. No printed words could approach the delight it was to sit across from him and listen to the lore that poured, somehow modestly, out of him.

Like all great athletes, Heffelfinger burned with an unquenchable desire to win at all cost. This was a phase of his character which he also carried out in life. He always played within the rules. But he had no rules as to the physical limit he would go for victory.

It was his essential love for the game and the battle that made him the great player that he was. Pudge loved football much more than the fame, adulation and awards it brought him.

"Football," he once told me philosophically, "is nothing more than a great *game* and not deserving of the hysteria and wildness it often creates." He meant it was a great contest of wills—not of talk.

I can be as pure in my praise of Pudge as the most bedraggled and worshipping fan who would pluck at his sleeve for his autograph. Take it from me, most of the legends that cluster around the magic name of Heffelfinger differ from all other legends of the Gay Nineties in that they are mostly true.

When I went to Yale the stories of Heff and all the greats were stuffed into me morning, noon and night by the Old Blues, then still a part of the local scene —returning each fall from all over the country. Yale football "belonged" to them.

Heff, as they told me, was never called Pudge by teammates. He was a large fellow—around two hundred pounds, I guess, a lot of it in his shoulders, arms and hands—when he arrived at New Haven in 1888. But there were complaints that he was too timid, which he wasn't. He was just respectful. One night he received a frightening letter suggesting he show more rough stuff or turn in his uniform. It was scribbled in blood, which had been obtained at a near-by slaughterhouse. That was the signal of freedom he welcomed. It was the Yale battle cry. You couldn't hold Pudge back after that.

Heffelfinger and Frank Hinkey, Yale's deceptive frail-looking end, 152 pounds, became twin centers of a legend that Pudge was the greatest blocking and running guard of all time and Hinkey the hardest tackler. This legend is part of the football story in America today.

My first meeting with Pudge was a rather violent one. It goes back to an afternoon at New Haven in 1916. I was the Yale quarterback that season. Pudge had been asked by Tad Jones to do some specialty line coaching. I was awed at the sight of him. There he was, a rawboned fellow, with arms that looked the size of stovepipes, powerful shoulders, huge hands, and a flaming spirit that spread all over the Bowl.

Heffelfinger, I said to myself. The great Heffelfinger. Talk about hero-worshippers. These fellows were far more important to us than Clark Gable and Spencer Tracy were to their fans. Heffelfinger . . . Stagg . . . Corbin . . . Hinkey . . . flaming legends rather than flesh and blood. Pudge was a "god" to all of us. There he was decked out in practice gear getting ready to scrimmage with the scrubs against us. But you know what happened. He roughed up our varsity line plenty. Cupid Black injured his leg, and Mac Baldridge suffered several broken ribs. Coach Tad Jones had to get Pudge out of there before he wrecked all of us—or we flattened him, for *no* one asked for quarter.

That story has been told often, but one thing is always left out. They never tell how tough Baldridge and Black were. Baldridge, as tough as they come, and despite his cracked-in side, wore a special chest protector and played against both Princeton and Harvard on successive Saturdays. And he played the whole 120 minutes and not one yard was made through him. And Cupe played every minute of both games, too—game leg and all!

Most of Pudge's stories about things unrelated to football, some of them beauts, concerned his experiences as a railroad hand in the Pacific Northwest just after he got out of college, and later in politics. Typical of his courage was the time he wandered into one of Montana's little mining towns, alone, and interrupted a lynching party. There must have been a thousand ranchers on hand. They had just hauled up this guy on the end of a rope and were watching him dangle. Pudge in a flash took out his hunting knife and waded right through the mob, daring anyone to try an' stop him. Nobody did. They knew better. Pudge cut down the fellow and escorted him out of there. Later, in court, he proved that the man was innocent all the time.

Not only was Pudge a great football star, he became a great citizen in his community as well. After a fling at coaching, he entered his father's shoe business in Minneapolis, later entered the real estate trade and built several of Minneapolis' leading office buildings. He was a delegate to the Republican National Conventions in 1904 and 1908, and served as chairman on the Hennepin County Commission for twenty-four years. Back in 1933, along with two partners, his nephew, Totten P. Heffelfinger, and Charles H. Pearson, Pudge organized Heffelfinger Publications and produced the first football guide. His famous "Football Facts" became a household word.

But Pudge's chief love was football. He personified the

real spirit of football more than anybody I have ever seen. His spirit shouldn't be allowed to die as his kind will never pass this way again. For Pudge set a pattern of high ideals that the game must follow if it is to survive. The game, as we know it, was born and brought up in the Heffelfinger manner. He carried it to all parts of the country. He kept the game in its proper perspective, always held that real football players didn't need and should not get any special favors. He just as firmly opposed any policy that discouraged good all-around athletes, who can do the academic work, from being welcomed at Ivy League schools. He felt they had an equal right to secure what scholarship aid was available and should not be discriminated against. He believed in all college teams consisting of representative undergraduates who are treated just the same as non-athletes. He was against the lowering of scholastic standards in any way.

Pudge felt Yale could follow these ideas and ideals and still play and lick anyone in the country. He never gave up that belief and hope. I know that he was proud that Princeton had kept alive the Ivy League tradition for valor and no quarter to anyone, and it was Pudge's conviction that Yale was finding the balance and attracting the kind of students who could stand up with any of the "bought and paid for" teams. And he was the happiest man on the field when Yale licked Princeton, 26-24, in 1953.

Just before the Big Game between Yale and Harvard in 1953, Pudge was given the National Football Hall of Fame Award. I am proud to have been the one chosen to

stand out there on the field before the kick-off and hand
it to him with the University Orator—Clair Mendell, Professor of Greek and Director of Athletics—and a Heff fan.
It made me think of the lines Grantland Rice once wrote,
which I have carried around in my pocket for thirty
years:

> With frame of iron and heart of steel,
>   You've earned a nation's cheers.
> You stand among the valiant few
>   Who've whipped the passing years.
> And may you wave forever, Pudge,
>   On through eternal space.
> To you—who helped to make the game
>   That helped to make our race!

Right up to the very end, football students continued
to go to Pudge for football advice. He seldom gave it to
them in words. Instead, he showed them. He spit on
his hands and crouched over and showed them how to
charge. "There ain't much to being a football player," he
told them, "if you're a football player."

When Yale meets Harvard each autumn, Pudge, in
body, no longer will be in his familiar spot in the stadium,
sitting near the Yale bench. But, he'll be there in spirit
next year and next and, for that matter, in the way Babe
Ruth has never left the Yankee Stadium, Pudge Heffelfinger will be wherever the Elis are playing forever.

He was a one man ARMY in himself—always ready to
take on one and all—a few or many—as long as they
would fight to the finish. As far as I know, he never lost a
battle . . . or even a skirmish.

A man is measured in the final analysis by the size of his soul.

John McCallum will prove to you that "giants" really lived. God's legions have their walking H-bomb now.

1

Granddaddy of the Old Blues

It has been said by some historians that I will go down as "the greatest football player of all time." It's always nice to read that sort of thing, but deep in my heart I know it isn't true. I can honestly claim, however, that I stuck with the game longer than anybody else did. On and off, I was an active football player for fifty years.

Maybe fifty years is too long a time to stick with a game, but I stayed in there because I loved football and body contact. It wasn't the headlines—they never meant much to me. I played football for the same reason that other middle-aged men play golf and tennis. Those are strenuous games, but they lacked something I wanted— the fierce elation that comes from throwing your body across an opponent's knees and feeling him hit the ground with a solid crack.

I'm no writer—that's why I asked John McCallum to put my story of football down on paper for me—or even an expert. But I've got one thing on my side no other football reporter or player has. That's perspective. I have always been able to size up the trends of football from

personal experience, because I played against the best of
the real old-timers and the great stars of the post World
War I era.

One thing I am certain about: Individual line play today isn't so effective as it was in the 1890's. Whenever I
see a bunch of modern linemen down on their knees like
stuffed bears in front of a fur shop, I wish I could lop
twenty years off my life and get back in there for some
more licks. In fact, twenty years ago, in the fall of 1933,
when I was nearing my sixty-sixth birthday, I came out
of the stands and played nine minutes of a charity game
in Minneapolis.

The game had been arranged between a graduate team
from St. Thomas College and a bunch of semi-profession-
als recruited by Ken Haycraft, former Minnesota end.
The advance ticket sale was terrible, and the promoters
feared a financial flop.

Ballyhoo was needed, and I was picked as the feature
attraction.

"Heff," they pleaded, "this game is going to lay an egg.
We need a darn-fool act to fire interest. You're it. Folks
will pay to see a sixty-five-year-old codger like you mix it
with a bunch of cocky kids."

"Not me," I protested. "I'll get hurt if I try to play with
this spare tire around my middle."

Well, they coaxed me into it by stressing how much the
wounded war veterans needed help.

When I got to the locker room they had no football
pants large enough to fit me. I pulled a jersey on over my
shirt, improvised hip pads by stuffing the pockets of my
ordinary business suit trousers with towels, borrowed a
helmet and went out to scrimmage with rough, rugged

kids young enough to be my grandsons. And, mind you, I had no kidney pads, no knee pads—no nothing!

The St. Thomas boys were a proud and confident lot. By golly, they didn't intend to be shown up by an old gaffer like me.

I didn't try any fancy stuff like pulling out of guard and running interference that afternoon—just bulled through. It was on one of those charges that I got hurt. While I was lying flat, a defensive man accidentally kicked me on the knee. It hurt a lot, and began to stiffen.

"Heff, you old fool," I said to myself, "this is as far as you go." I told the referee to hold it, that I had finally got some sense and was quitting voluntarily after nine minutes. That was the first and only time I ever left a game without orders from the bench.

(McCallum in for Heffelfinger: Deep in this vein, Tiny Thornhill, the old Stanford coach, tells of the time he and Pudge played together at guards in an All-Star game. On a mass play, Pudge was hurt, but got up to continue.

"Sorry, Tiny," he said, after three blockers had charged over him, "I wasn't much help to you on that last play. My right leg wouldn't work. Maybe it's broken."

It was, yet it took seven burly teammates to force him on to a stretcher and off the field.)

Looking back on my fifty years as an active performer, I find the games you lose are the ones you can't forget. Victories fade, but defeats bite their way into your heart and stick there like gum to the floor.

I never did like to lose. Fortunately, I was always associated with winning teams, both at Yale and later in my forty years of football barnstorming. But the few drubbings we suffered—they're the ones I have never been able to forget. Take, for instance, the only time Harvard beat us in my four years at New Haven. I still play one particular maneuver over in my dreams.

This was in 1890 and the score was 12-0 against us when we began to roll and pushed Bum McClung over for a touchdown after a long march. I ran interference a few minutes later for Ben Morison on an end run that ate up forty yards. He was loose, with me ahead of him and two Harvard tacklers closing in—Bernie Trafford in front of us and Dudley Dean behind.

Quick, which Crimson man should I take out? Dean was moving up rapidly from the rear and I went for him, figuring that Morison could dodge Trafford. I was wrong. Trafford nailed him and we were dead ducks.

I have played that one over in my sleep many a night, and I always take out Trafford!

Funny, isn't it, how such a trivial incident can get a man? Our Captain Rhodes was so heartbroken over this defeat that he never would look at another Harvard-Yale game. Years later he would pace the lobby of the old Massasoit House in Springfield with a ticket in his pocket while the game was being played.

It seems that in those days we thought there was a divine law against a Yale football team losing. Come to think of it, we lost only two games in my four years. Princeton trimmed us in 1889, when the great Hector Cowan and Snake Ames wore the Orange and Black.

That was my first loss at Yale and I didn't want to show my face on the campus. I remember sneaking upstairs to my room, locking the door, and not saying a word when some of my chums shouted for me. It sounds

silly now, but kids were like that in the not so Gay
Nineties.

Today—well, today the boys seem to be more interested in scholarship and board deals than in "dying for
dear old Rutgers."

I've never claimed to be the greatest guard of my generation, let alone of all time. But when it comes to running interference I won't take a back seat for anybody.
Nobody has ever had anything on me as an open-field
blocker from the guard position—I was the first guard to
run interference, you know. It was while benched with a
shoulder injury that I got the bright idea of a guard pulling out of the line to run interference.

I was pretty fast for my size, 6-foot-2, 188 pounds, and
I sprang the play against Pennsylvania by pivoting out of
the line, taking three strides to the right, and turning in
ahead of the ball carrier outside the defensive tackle. The
maneuver crushed the Quakers, 32-0.

I think if the late Bo McMillin were still with us, he
would back me up on my downfield-blocking boasts. The
great Indiana coach will be best remembered as the rab-
bitlike quarterback of the dazzling Centre College team
which beat Harvard in 1921. Bo was quick on the get-
away, and his specialty was flanking the short-side end
on reverse plays.

I blocked for McMillin in a charity game at Columbus,
in 1922, just after he graduated from Centre College. We
were playing for a pick-up team from all over the map
against a bunch of Ohio State grads. I was fifty-four
years old. Practically all the others were fresh out of
school.

We had quite a team. Slippery Eddie Casey, of Harvard, and Notre Dame's Ray Eichenlaub, a pile-driving line buster, played alongside McMillin in our all-star backfield. Centre College's Red Roberts, a whale of an end, was used at blocking back that day because he had the weight and speed to smear tacklers.

Great as our squad shaped up on paper, the Ohio State grads were hot favorites. The Buckeye backfield featured household Columbus names—Chick Harley, Pete Stinchcomb and Noel Workman. Harley was a greater all-around back than Red Grange because he could do more things well. Names like Trott, Nemecek and Huffman stood out in the Scarlet and Gray line.

I was elected captain, and I insisted on playing a balanced line. Unbalanced lines have been the vogue in more recent years, but I have always argued that you can put on a more versatile two-way attack when there are three men on each side of center.

McMillin, our quarterback, didn't exactly like the idea of having a rheumatic old gent up there in the line. He said it was a press-agent gag, and he didn't bother to hide his feelings.

"I understand each college will start a man and that you represent Yale," Bo said to me in the dressing room before the game. "I thought this game was for blood, not a reunion of old-timers. I came up here to win!"

I eyed him acidly.

"What do you think brought me to Columbus?" I growled. "I've played football to win for thirty years, and if I find I can't deliver out there today I'll take myself out."

They made me wear a headguard. Back in the nineties we played bareheaded—let our hair grow long to prevent scalp cuts. I never got dazed by a blow on the head in four years at Yale. Certain folks have hinted that maybe my skull was too thick.

We had only about ten plays, but we beat the Ohio State grads, 16-0. Some modern teams can't score with even seventy plays—they're all snarled up in their own web of signals.

Four of our ten plays were forward passes. Eddie Casey grabbed one thrown by McMillin and raced to a touchdown. He sure could change pace. Sheer speed isn't worth a hoot unless you apply it in bursts. Stop-go runners are the fellows who fake the tackler into bow knots.

I helped McMillin break loose on our second touchdown, a fifty-yard run, just outside tackle. I took out the Ohio State end. McMillin was amazed to see "the old man" lead him. Bo was a quick starter, but by timing my getaway to the dot I covered those four spaces in three strides and turned in ahead of him to ride my opponent wide.

I was getting along okay until I rammed into an opposing blocker while going down under a punt. The impact conked my shoulder out of its socket. The doctor came out and snapped my shoulder into place, then he took my arm to lead me toward the sideline. I shoved him away, then started back to my position.

"Where're you going?" he asked curtly.

"I didn't come in to play twenty minutes," I said. "I'm going to see this job through."

I almost made good that boast. They let me stay in there for fifty-one minutes. Then my feet began to drag a bit and I didn't object very hard when they sent in a substitute.

The more moderns claim it is exhausting for a boy to play sixty minutes. Bunk! Any properly trained youngster can go sixty minutes without suffering any bad after-effects. We did it week after week, and football was just as fast a game in the nineties, even though we had no forward pass.

Did you know that the ball is actually in play for only twelve minutes in a sixty-minute football game? Stop-watch tests will support this statement. Why should a football player be leg weary after only twelve minutes' action? It makes me laugh!

Listen. In 1892, fresh out of Yale, I barnstormed with the Chicago Athletic Club football team. We played six games in twelve days! That's right, and we had only twelve players.

We started the tour off in Cleveland, beating the day-lights out of Case School. The following afternoon we were knocking heads with Syracuse. Two of our men had suffered injuries in the Case game, so we recruited the Syracuse coach, Bert Hanson, to play center for us. In the huddle, Hanson revealed all his boys' plays. We mur-dered 'em.

Borrowing three men from the Boston Athletic Club, we lost the next day to Harvard.

Pennsylvania was the next stop. The two teams were secondary in this one. The officials were the whole show. The referee favored Penn, the umpire us. We just stood there as, first, the referee would walk off a penalty against us, only to see the umpire charge in, pick up the ball, and pace off a penalty against the Quakers. It developed into quite a seesaw contest. I don't recall who won.

After Pennsylvania came Princeton. Sport Donnelly, the

old Tiger star, playing left end for us, refused to play against his alma mater. That left us with only ten men, so we played with one man short. Another Princeton grad, Snake Ames, agreed to play for us that afternoon, but I'm afraid loyalty to the Orange and Black kept him from putting his heart into his work.

We traveling canvasbacks finished the tour beating the Crescent Athletic Club in Brooklyn, making it six games in twelve days. It was amateur football at its best—amateur in every sense of the word. We didn't even get traveling expenses!

But look at all the fun we had.

Sport Donnelly was a card during those barnstorming days. His idea of humor was to punch his opponent in the nose, and then yell, "Hey, Mr. Referee!" The official usually looked around just in time to see Donnelly take a return blow on the jaw. Naturally the supposed aggressor was ejected, while Donnelly chuckled.

Donnelly pulled this trick in one of our games and the opposing end—a Pittsburgh ex-cop—kicked Donnelly in the ribs as Sport lay on the ground. Somebody blew a riot whistle. The police swarmed in and arrested their former buddy.

The ex-cop was the only football player I ever saw carted away from the field in a patrol wagon!

2

Rocks of the Ages

On and off, as I have said, I was an active football player for fifty years. I started as a fifteen-year-old schoolboy in my home town of Minneapolis, when Rugby had just been modified to suit our Yankee yen for knocking people down. I ended as a tired old man of sixty-five in a charity game at Minneapolis against kids young enough to be my grandsons.

I've been a grandstand gawker for quite a few years now and eligible for membership to the downtown quarterbacks' club. Well, you can't say I didn't serve a long apprenticeship and earn my card in the Knockers' Union.

It's human to criticize, I guess. But when I hear some brass-lunged, raccoon-coated old grad yell "Bonehead!" at a college quarterback, I feel like saying, "Buster, could you call 'em right every time if you were out there getting your brains knocked down your throat?"

Second-guessers can be cruel. They should think twice before blighting a boy's career with epithets. I have in mind Denny Clark, the "goat" of the 1905 Michigan-Chicago game, who was thrown for a safety while trying to run one of Walter Eckersall's punts out from behind Michigan's goal line. Catlin, of Chicago, hit Clark just as he reached the line and dragged him back. Chicago won, 2-0, on this break. Stung by the taunts of "Bonehead!" Clark quit Ann Arbor and hid away in Michigan's north woods. For years he lived more or less as a recluse. Ironically, Denny might have raced one hundred yards for a touchdown, had he dodged that Chicago tackler, and emerged a hero. There was an open lane down the east side line.

Ken Sandbach, of Princeton, almost pulled a Denny Clark against Yale in 1934. He caught the Eli kick in his own end zone and foolishly fought his way through several Yale tacklers, barely reaching the one-yard mark. Sandbach would have saved twenty yards for Princeton simply by touching the ball down. The Eli tacklers were equally scatterbrained—they tried their best to nail Sandbach before he could reach the field of play.

Football annals are studded with classic bonehead plays—abrupt twists defying explanation that transformed potential stars into something more like cap-and-bell buffoons.

Bonehead, dumbbell, boob—those are samples of the epithets showered upon the unhappy young athletes who do the wrong thing or leave the right undone in time of crisis. The amazing thing, in a game as hard-hitting and fierce as football, is that there are not more slip-ups—kids going the wrong way after untangling from a pile-up, et cetera.

On two occasions against Dartmouth during the two-platoon era, Army lined up to kick the extra point with only ten men on the field. Frank Wilkerson forgot he was a two-way tackle and ran off the field with the offensive unit.

Coach Amos Alonzo Stagg laughs fit to be tied telling how a Susquehanna lineman, suddenly transferred from the scrubs to the varsity, wheeled around in a scrimmage session when the substitutes kicked, and leveled his own ball-carrier.

Many a combatant besides Roy Riegels, the California center who immortalized himself in 1929 by running seventy yards the wrong way against Georgia Tech in the Rose Bowl, has galloped in the wrong direction. Whitey Thomas, Princeton center, ran ten yards toward his own goal after recovering a fumble in the 1919 Yale game. He would have gone all the way if Maury Trimble, a Tiger halfback, hadn't spilled him with a flying tackle.

"No wonder centers run the wrong way," chortled Bob Zuppke, the old Illinois coach. "They spend all their time looking at the world upside down."

Snooks Dowd of Lehigh set the fashion in the rock-'em-sock-'em nineties, but his adventure had a happy ending. After dashing fifty yards toward his own goal and crossing it, Dowd suddenly discovered his error, wheeled abruptly, and ran the length of the field for a touchdown. He was just out for the exercise. They hailed Dowd as the originator of the double reverse after that one, and he became a slick strategist instead of a rockhead.

Years ago, House Janeway, Princeton guard, discovered that when the Yale quarterback pinched his center on the leg, the latter snapped the ball. Janeway tipped off Sport Donnelly, Tiger end, to expect a fumble. On the next play, Janeway reached over the Yale line and surreptitiously pinched the center. At the bogus signal the pivot snapped the ball before his backs were ready, Donnelly slid through, picked up the fumble, and scooted for a touchdown.

Not all boners are pulled on the field. In the fall of 1951, a West Virginia scout took notes as keenly-tooled Maryland crushed North Carolina State, 53-0. The Mountaineers were next for the vaunted Terrapins. The scout was asked to compare the two teams.

"West Virginia," he said, "makes too many mistakes to be a formidable opponent for Maryland."

Mistakes? What, for instance?

"Scheduling Maryland," he replied.

Modern football demands quicker thinking by the defensive backs than the old game did, because they must watch for forward passes. I like the pass. But just as the infantry remains the "Queen of Battle," despite the airplane, so the rushing game is still the keystone of a sound attack. The pass, a supplementary weapon, is often overdone.

Knute Rockne believed that the issue was decided in the line—"up front where the game is," as he would flatly put it. The Notre Dame lines of 1929 and 1930, in my opinion, came nearest to matching the great Yale lines of 1888 and 1891 in technique and speed off the mark. Rockne taught his linemen to stand up on defense, slide laterally with the play, and fan off blockers by vigorous though legal use of hands. Their heads were up so they could see what was happening.

In general, those old Yale lines were faster than our modern barriers. In my day every lineman was fast enough to be a ball carrier as well. In fact, when I began playing football as a schoolboy of fifteen, on the Minneapolis sandlots, in 1883, I imagined myself as being something of a ball carrier. And, later, when I reported for football in 1888 at old Yale Field, where the baseball diamond now sprawls, a friend of mine had tipped off Kid Wallace, freshman coach and varsity end, that I was a crack running halfback. Wallace gave me a chance on the freshman team.

Pa Corbin, varsity captain, happened to be watching freshman practice when I caught a punt off my shoe tops and ran through all the opposition except "Tot" Harvey. They played fifteen-man sides to give us dodging experience, and the sky was raining tacklers.

Luck plus ability spells success. If Corbin hadn't seen that run I might have spent all season on the yearling team. Freshmen were eligible for the varsity then. Moreover, the Yale varsity captain outranked the coach. He could pick his own team and decide what plays to use. The coach was just an adviser.

Pa Corbin's long face and handlebar mustache gave him a majestic air, and made him look much older than his twenty-four years. His word was law on Yale Field, in 1888.

"Hey, you freshman, come over here!" the Great Man ordered, after seeing my run. My heart beat a tattoo as I ran over.

"Nice run," Pa grunted. "Ever play in the line?"

"No," I stammered.

"Well, come over to the varsity field with me," Corbin commanded, "and see what you can do at guard. You're big and fast. We need linemen more than backs. Have you any nickname?"

"No," I lied, remembering that my dad disliked my

school nickname, Pudge, and had warned me not to use it at Yale.

"Fine," said Corbin, "we'll call you 'Heff.' Your real name is too long."

As "Heff" I made the Yale varsity line on my first day out. I never again played in the backfield after leaving prep school. They gave you a rough initiation in those days. I took plenty that afternoon, particularly from Bert Hanson. Playing opposite me in scrimmage, he alternately kicked my shins and cracked my knuckles. Pa Corbin would vary this occasionally by rasping the sleeve of his canvas jacket across my nose until it was raw.

"Let's see if he's got any guts!" Kid Wallace shouted.

They gave me the ball and sent three men down to crack me simultaneously. One tackler took me high around the neck, another hit me in the belly, and the third went for my hips.

They seemed satisfied with everything except my tackling.

"You're too good-natured, Heff," Ray Tompkins warned me. "You've got to be mean to play on this team, and you must bang 'em down hard."

I got rough. From that day on, I played as if I wanted to kill my opponent. That freshman experience stuck. But the story doesn't stop there. Just before the United States got into World War I, I played against the 1916 Yale line while coaching at New Haven. Captain Cupid Black was at guard, Tim Callahan played center, Gates and Baldridge were the tackles. I was forty-eight years old, but, thanks to my stand-up stance, I could start quicker than any of the youngsters. I was still hard as nails and liked to mix it up.

When the varsity stars saw me take my place in the scrub line they said to one another, "Let's show the old boy up."

"Go easy with him," cautioned Coach Tad Jones. "Remember, he's an old man."

I knew that if I was to get their respect as a line coach I'd have to lick them physically. Kids will take advice if you show 'em you've got the stuff. They lined up opposite me with tolerant amusement. Black and Baldridge, I could see, had decided to double-team me. I beat 'em to the charge, knocked them both flying and spilled the play for a loss. I did this a second time and a third time.

Black limped over to the sidelines, and said to Coach Jones, "This old guy's roughing us up. Why can't we fight back?"

"Go ahead and fight back," Jones said.

On the very next play I drove Black into Baldridge. Black weighed 210 pounds and was built like a coke oven. He fell on top of Baldridge, breaking two of the latter's ribs. Black went over to Jones again, a badly bruised and chastened young man.

"Get that old so and so off the field," he said. "He's ruining our team."

And that's how the story you still hear got started that I had wrecked the 1916 varsity line—with the Princeton game only a week away and the Harvard game a week after that!

The Yales of '16, incidentally, were the first from New Haven to beat a Harvard team coached by the great Percy Haughton. The victory came after eight straight years of frustration. This in itself distinguishes the Yales of '16 in the history of Eli football.

The advance preparation for that game was really something. In those days, Percy used to arm his linemen with skintight gloves of hard leather which reached well up the forearm. This was purportedly to protect the linemen's hands and wrists. But the effect on the opposing linemen was not at all pleasant—like being struck by a pair of brass knuckles.

Well, the day before the Big Game Coach Jones called on Coach Haughton and told him he had ordered a similar set of gloves for the Yales—which was the truth—and that if he insisted on using the leather coverings Yale was going to use them, too.

"Why, if you feel we shouldn't use the gloves," said Percy, "we just won't use them. I never knew you had the slightest objection. . . ."

Tad assured him Yale had a very positive objection, and so the equipment was discarded by both sides.

Tad, I might add, didn't tell Percy anything about the plaster of Paris cast he was making Larry Fox, one of his stars, wear on his right hand for the game. Larry was supposed to have a bad hand, but there was nothing wrong with it. When Fox hit one of those Harvards with that cast the guy would drop like a ton of brick.

Them wuz the days.

During the first World War, I served as draft-board commissioner and Red Cross worker, so I didn't get back to New Haven until the fall of 1920. Tad Jones had just been reappointed head coach. I phoned him that I was at his disposal in scrimmage workouts. An hour later he met me at the hotel.

"We've been talking things over, Heff," he said, "and we've decided not to let you put on a suit this year."

Well, I thought that was all right. He was afraid I'd get hurt. I'd been out of Yale for thirty years, and I was getting kind of old, and it wouldn't be a good thing for football if I got hurt. It wouldn't look right.

"All right, Tad," I said, "I appreciate your thoughtfulness. You're afraid I might get hurt."

"That's not it," replied Jones. "We are afraid you might hurt some of our boys. We're short of linemen as it is."

"Is that so?" I said. "Well, if that's the kind of players you have, I don't want to have anything to do with them."

I got on a train and went right back to Minneapolis. I never went back to New Haven to coach again. Funny thing, as a freshman, back in 1888, they warned me I couldn't hold my job unless I showed more viciousness in practice.

"Heff, you remind me of a big cow," Pa Corbin would growl. "You're too easygoing and good-natured. Rattle their teeth on every tackle after this or turn in your jersey. Friendship ceases when the whistle blows."

I kept my varsity job by obeying Corbin's orders, but thirty-two years later I was barred from a Yale scrimmage as being too rough!

Times change.

3

The Big Three

You've got to play football for all there's in it, or somebody who hits harder will send you off on a stretcher. In my time we never wasted time tackling the dummy. Our workouts stressed live tackling, man against man in the open field. This is what made us real tacklers.

There was none of that pawing and tagging you see so frequently today. You can't learn how to nail a flesh-and-blood moving target by tackling a straw-stuffed dummy.

I used to lose four or five pounds in scrimmage. Game days seemed like a vacation to us. On Sunday we took six-mile hikes across country. Rockne once said that football was 60 per cent leg drive and 30 per cent fight. We had both.

We had about five hundred students watching practice each afternoon. The students felt that they were part of the team. That intimate tie no longer exists. Your sophisticated young modern sneers at the rah-rah spirit as we knew it. But it remains the stuff of which great football teams are made. In my time the students yelled at you during practice and called you a bum after the workout if you missed a block or tackle. This kept us on our toes.

Don't get the idea this is going to be totally an Ivy

League story. It isn't. I will touch on the whole American scene before I'm through, but since college football really started with the Big Three—Yale, Harvard and Princeton —perhaps I should continue in that vein.

Pa Corbin's 1888 team, for example, ranks near the top in Yale's history. We ran up 698 points to 0 for our opponents. Giants? Don't make me laugh! I was the heaviest man on our team at 188 pounds, not exactly gargantuan as some historians would have you believe. Alonzo Stagg, then better known as a baseball pitcher than as an end, weighed only 157 pounds. We were hard as nails, and fast. There was absolutely nothing ponderous about us.

George Woodruff and I flanked Pa Corbin in the middle of the line. Woodruff wore a coonskin cap and sported a set of whiskers when he first came to Yale from a Pennsylvania Dutch homestead. He broke all strength-test records at New Haven. I envied Woodruff's whiskers and vainly tried to sprout a crop of my own.

Alonzo Stagg, later to become synonymous with University of Chicago football, was a twenty-seven-year-old Divinity School student when he played end for us. For all his biblical precepts, Lon was the foxiest of gridiron tacticians. He thought two plays ahead of the other fellow, like a master surveying a chessboard.

Stagg organized a barnstorming team called the Christian Workers of Springfield, Massachusetts, after the college season each fall. The "dead man" was one of his pet trick plays. When the ball was snapped, the whole team would run toward the left flank, as though on an end run, except the chap who took the pass from center. He flopped on his stomach with the ball concealed beneath him—and played dead. When the enemy players rushed over to stop the fake end sweep, the corpse jumped to his feet and was off to the races. It was a rather unchristian play, but, by golly, it accounted for a lot of touchdowns.

Kid Wallace played opposite end from Stagg. He was a good-natured hellion who kept us laughing with his rowdy antics. A gentleman to the manner born, Wallace delighted in pretending to be a brawler of the Pier 6 type. Football was just an excuse for swapping punches, as far as Wallace was concerned. But his wit turned away wrath. He could sock you and laugh it off with a wisecrack. A grim, serious gang like ours needed comic relief. The Kid supplied it.

Lee McClung, a freshman like myself, was a spirited Southerner with a puzzling hip shift and a scissors stride that baffled tacklers. I've seen many superb open-field runners since I played alongside Bum McClung sixty-two years ago, but, except for George Gipp, Win Osgood and Red Grange, I've never looked at McClung's equal.

Ever hear of Win Osgood? The modern generation doesn't recognize the name, yet the Pennsylvania star was the nearest thing to Grange as a broken-field runner I've seen. Tall, blond, broad-shouldered and lean-hipped, he would have pleased Praxiteles as a sculptor's model. My old friend, the late George Trevor, onetime Yale historian, once described Osgood as "a picture of rhythmic motion, a smooth, effortless runner, always in balance." Osgood didn't dodge tacklers or bull through them. Instead, he evaded them by a slight twist of the torso. It was downright uncanny to watch him run down the middle of the

field, scarcely deviating from a straight course, while opponents missed him by inches. His body undulated like
a snake's.

Osgood was a born crusader. It was no surprise when
he joined the Cuban Insurrection against Spanish tyr-
anny. Typical was the way he exposed himself reck-
lessly under fire to hearten his men. A bullet drilled him
through the forehead as he rode his horse toward a Spanish blockhouse. Eyewitnesses say that Osgood's body remained upright in the saddle for many seconds after his
fearless spirit had taken wing.

Billy Bull, 1888 Yale fullback, has had few superiors at
kicking. He would punt on the run with either foot, like a
Rugby player, and his drop-kicks sometimes scored from
forty yards out.

Doc Wurtenberg, our little 1888 quarterback, had to
handle the ball on every play under the old rules, but he
didn't call signals. Numerical signals weren't invented
until 1890. Pa Corbin employed signs to let us know what
play he wanted. When he yanked his cap visor, that
meant a kick. Any move of his left hand implied a play in
that direction. Corbin signaled a plunge over guard by
tugging at his belt, and an end run by touching his shoe-
lace. Our opponents never got wise.

Back there at the beginning, the Princeton-Yale game
ended the season. Princeton's V—a wedge of men which
had smashed every defense it had met—was a terrible
thing to face. It simply mowed down the men up front
like wooden soldiers. The man at the apex put the ball in
play, and the runner was screened by the phalanx. We
met the lead man by socking him in the jaw with the heel
of the hand. But they rolled over us just the same.

Then an idea socked me like a flying bottle in a bowery pub. Why not fight fire with fire? As the wedge formed, I backed away to get a running start, put on full steam ahead, took off like a broad jumper, knees doubled up, and soared. I crashed against the chest of the guy leading the V. The impact caused the wedge to shiver and collapse.

"Hey," thundered Hector Cowan, a chunky, deep-chested fellow, built like a smokehouse, "you want somebody to get kilt!"

"I'll quit it if you stop using that V wedge," I said. They refused, then foxed me by ducking low and warding off my dive with upflung arms. Luck was with me, though, on one critical play when I spotted a gap in the V and went shooting through there to nail Snake Ames for a big loss. That spoiled a Princeton scoring drive.

Neither side scored a touchdown that afternoon, but we won, 10-0, on Billy Bull's drop-kicks. I can see him now, booting the first field goal with blood streaming down his face from a scalp wound. We wore no helmets or harness. Bull's second field goal was booted from a sharp angle on the thirty-seven-yard line with barely a minute left to play.

We actually had two head coaches at Yale in 1888— Walter Camp and his earnest young wife. She was her husband's eyes. They were newlyweds that year and Walter had just gone to work for a New Haven clock company. His boss wouldn't let him attend our practice sessions, but he kept in touch with everything that happened by reading his wife's notebook.

Mrs. Camp used to pace the sideline, jotting down notes. She could spot the good points and weaknesses in each man's play. Her woman's intuition helped Walter suggest the right man for each position to the captain. In those days the coach made no decision without consulting the captain.

Talk about the 1888 Princeton game being rough. You should have been on hand to see us play Harvard the following year. We played at old Hampden Park in Springfield, Massachusetts. Why Springfield? Well, in those days the Big Three games were played on neutral grounds. Princeton-Yale was at the Polo Grounds in New York, about halfway from each campus, you see. Springfield was about seventy-five miles from New Haven and one hundred miles from Boston, which made it a good spot for Harvard and Yale to meet. From 1889 to 1894 the games were played there. Bleachers were put up especially for the game. Tremendous crowd—fifteen thousand.

Another thing about Springfield was that it was a big railroad junction for New England. That's how the railroad station was wrecked one night. The Williams team and its rooters used to change cars at Springfield going to and from Yale for the annual game. Yale used to slaughter them. All the football there was of any class in those days was played by the Big Three. But this year the Williams rooters on the way back from New Haven were wild with delight. Why? Well, Yale won by the usual fifty or one hundred points—but Williams had scored! Yes, sir, Williams had scored on mighty Yale and the Williams crowd on the way back was so exuberant it just about tore down the Springfield railroad station. It was a public benefit at that. Springfield needed a new one.

But to get back to the Yale-Harvard game of '89, I

could rattle off the line-ups of both teams right now if I had to. I can see those Traffords in their Harvard uniforms, and what uniforms they had in those days. Cumnock was the Harvard captain and Charley Gill was the Yale leader. Stagg played right end. I remember after the game a woodcut caricature of Lon handing one of the Harvard chaps a right good wallop on the head and the caption was "Stagg's Ministerial Uppercut." It was in one of the Springfield papers.

The players would all get out there and murder one another for sixty minutes and after the game they would agree that there had been no slugging by either side. It was some battle—and the word "battle" is used advisedly. The slaughter was so terrific it was a wonder any of us came out alive. One of the Harvards had his collarbone broken. A Yale player had one eye nearly blinded. Practically all the players were bleeding from cuts or from kicks or smashes in the general mauling. Another one of our fellows was unconscious for five hours afterward in a Springfield hospital.

I don't remember now exactly who it was, but I can still see him being carried off the field. They just dumped him in a pile of blankets, covered him up, and then turned to look at the game again. A bit later, just out of curiosity, one of our subs went over and lifted the blankets apart and looked in. There he was, still unconscious—and nobody was paying any attention to him! They were all wrapped up in the game. So the sub covered him up again and went to have another look at the game himself.

Oh, yes, Yale won the game, 6-0. It was McClung who scored the touchdown and kicked the goal. In those days, you had to kick the goal from a point in front of where the touchdown had gone over the line. The Yale touchdown had been made over at one side of the field and I'm telling you that William Tell couldn't have shot an arrow through the goal posts from that angle, but McClung kicked the goal just the same!

My senior season, in 1891, found Yale with another great team—even stronger, in my opinion, than the '89 bunch. Captain McClung was a leader who never allowed us to consider the possibility of defeat. We rolled up 478 points to zero for the opposition. At end that year we had a scrawny, sunken-eyed, deathly pale little hellcat named Frank Hinkey.

Hinkey was the all-time football freak. He weighed only 152 pounds and looked anemic, a real runt among those bloomin' giants. Moreover, he wore no helmet or noseguard or shinguard or padding at all. He just plowed in there with no protection but what his pants and jersey afforded, and what he did to those upholstered Amazons was joyful to behold. He knocked 'em kicking and threw them head over heels.

Nobody ever made a first down around Hinkey's end all the time he played for Yale. Pound for pound, he was the fightingest bird I ever saw. In '94, the Harvard team was sent on the field with only two instructions. The first was to get that Hinkey out of there and the second was to win the game.

The Harvards tried hard enough and were pretty good men, but they didn't follow instructions. They didn't win the game. Yale won, 12-4. As for getting Hinkey out of there, why, he never had time taken out for him once during his college career. Never once!

Hinkey folded up like an accordion when he tackled his man—whipsawed the runner to earth with a cracking jolt that left the latter gasping for wind. I don't blame Harvard and Princeton men for being frightened of Hinkey—we were plenty scared of him ourselves when his lips narrowed to a thin line and his deep-set eyes glowed like live coals.

We called Hinkey "the silent end." He was a morose, introspective type, given to brooding spells. He seldom uttered a sound, never laughed at our jokes, took out his repressions on the football field. But, boy, was he rough. Opponents couldn't believe that such a little runt could tackle so dawgone hard. He wasn't particularly fast, but he seemed to have a nose for the ball. He really had football instinct, always anticipated plays intuitively and bobbed up at the crucial moment to recover fumbles miraculously. Do you know what Walter Camp used to say? He used to say that Hinkey "drifted through interference like a disembodied spirit." Frank lugged that football around with him on the campus and, until some professor made him quit, even took it along to the lecture room.

In my senior year against Harvard, a Crimson man gave Hinkey an uppercut under the jaw.

"My friend," said Hinkey, pointing to the aggressor, "if you hit me that hard again you will break your hand!"

This comeback was typical of the little chunk of nuclear energy.

Next to Frank Hinkey, George Foster Sanford was our most interesting recruit in '91. "Sandy" talked a marvelous game and then went out and delivered.

"I'm your center!" I remember Sandy announcing the first day he reported as a raw freshman. "I'll lick any bloke you send against me." He did, too, and he went on to become the school's stormy petrel.

"There's no king but Dodo!" he exclaimed at a conference of Yale coaches in 1909. He was then the line coach, and added, "When I walk out of this room I'll take Yale's offensive line play with me."

This threat was prompted by a disagreement between Camp and Sanford on line strategy. Sandy felt that Camp had been weaned away from the old Yale creed by misguided advisers. Tact wasn't Sandy's forte, but you couldn't fault his coaching. He specialized in keying his players to a fighting frenzy. What a job he did on Charley Chadwick in 1897. Chadwick, a regular big buster of a guy, was an easy-going chap who didn't know his own strength. He let the scrubs shove him around in scrimmage, was finally demoted to the reserves just before the Princeton game. Sandy took Chadwick aside on the morning of the game.

"Charley," he said, man to man, "I've heard that Princeton thinks you're yellow. They plan to run right over your position. Some of the Yale coaches think the same, but I've still got faith in you. If I start you this afternoon, could you stop 'em?"

"Let me at 'em!" roared Chadwick.

Sandy took no chances. He instructed the Yale center to slap Chadwick's face the first time the team lined up. The center did. Chadwick thought a Princeton man had slapped him and he went wild, ripping the Tiger line to shreds. Sanford chuckled on the bench.

Dick Harlow, who coached at Colgate back in the middle 1920's, was another master football psychologist. Ever hear what he did in 1924? Listen. He had a pharmacist

make up some harmless sugar pills just before the opening game. Then he called his team together for a secret
locker-room meeting.

"Fellas," he said, in hushed tones, taking the pills out
of his pocket, "these tablets are made from an old Indian
formula that I found in Pennsylvania. They give you tons
of strength. But keep it quiet, don't tell anybody we've
got 'em. Each one of you take a pill before the game starts
and we'll murder these guys."

The gullible Colgate players made a shambles of the
opposition that afternoon and flexed their muscles and
threw out their chests like Atlas. Harlow patted his bottle
of capsules and tapped a finger against his lips.

"Remember, keep this quiet," he whispered. The Ma-
roon players could hardly wait for their next "shot" the
following Saturday.

"Coach," they panted, "give us those pills."

They swamped Clarkson Tech, 41-0.

Then came the big trip to Lincoln to play mighty
Nebraska. Getting a glimpse of the hulking Cornhusk-
ers in practice, the Colgate players were awed. They felt
a bit queasy.

"Better double the dose, coach!" they told Harlow in
the dressing room before the game. Dick doled out two
pills apiece.

Despite the extra "shot," Colgate was trampled, 33-7.
The visitors eyed their coach dubiously.

"Coach," they inquired, "what went wrong with the
pills?" Harlow forced a laugh.

"Men," he said, "those were just plain sugar pills. Football is all in the mind!"

4

The Masters

You hear talk about "giving the game back to the boys," but football offense has become so complex that the kids wouldn't know what to do with the game if they got it.

Kee-ripes, how different modern football is from the old days when the coach wouldn't dare make a decision without first consulting the team captain.

Your head coach today has become an absolute dictator. He not only picks the team, designs the plays and relegates the captain to a corporal's status—sometimes abolishing the captaincy altogether—but during the game, he frequently governs the choice of plays by remote control.

Sideline coaching, it says here, is illegal, but do you think coaches wear white gloves on the bench just to keep their hands warm? Watch the so-called field generals glance toward the bench when in doubt!

A number of years ago, I recollect a certain big-time coach used to warm up a player on the sideline as an animated signal. If the situation called for Play No. 22, the player wearing this numeral paraded at the coach's order until the quarterback out on the field caught on. The substitute always sat down again after warming up.

The scout of a midwestern team once pointed out to his boss that the opposing coach was fingering his hat whenever he wanted a pass thrown.

"Why don't you protest?" the scout wanted to know.

"Because," the head man said, "I'd rather play against the coach's judgment than against his quarterback's."

If I had my way, coaches would be isolated in the press box, once a game began. I'd let the captain run the works with a free hand, plan his own strategy and make substitutions. Maybe the game wouldn't be a technical masterpiece, but at least it would be a sporting battle of wits between college youngsters—which it was intended to be!

I can hear Gil Dobie disparaging that suggestion right now. Gloomy Gil, they called him, one of the really super coaches of the early days. He was a genuine perfectionist and couldn't imagine the kids ever running themselves. In fact, he always appeared to take a sadistic delight in belittling his own players' ability.

Football coaches have always been practicing pessimists, but Dobie was the king of them all. If you think Frank Leahy was gloomy, why, he was a regular ball of sunshine compared to the man who brought Cornell to the Ivy League peak during the early 1920's. Cornell went undefeated for three seasons, and after wrapping up the '23 campaign a reporter rushed up to Gloomy Gil and pumped his hand enthusiastically.

"Congratulations on a great team," the journalist said. Dobie stared at the newsman coldly.

"If this is a great team," he said, "then the human race must be degenerating!"

Whether or not Dobie's outward manner was a pose, his theory was that by predicting the worst, he could make himself appear something of a genius if his boys won, while if they lost that was only what should have been expected.

The shrewd Scotsman had cause to be gloomy in the late 1920's. His material soured and his caustic psychology was too much for the new kids. Cornell's football fortunes hit the skids.

The Big Red reached rock bottom when Pennsylvania drubbed them, 49-0.

"Gee, coach, wasn't that sad?" someone asked Dobie after the clobbering.

"Sad!" retorted the Gloomy One. "You don't know what sorrow is—wait till next year!"

"Anyway," the guy said, trying to console the Old Master, "it's still a treat to see your teams in action. Nobody else can teach backs to start so fast."

"That's the trouble," said Dobie dryly. "They get to the tacklers too soon!"

When the old Notre Dame star, Hughie Devore, was coaching at New York University and things were going from bad to worse, it was suggested he try Dobie's psychology

"I wouldn't dare tell my kids how bad they are," said Devore. "They'd believe me."

To find a modern counterpart of Dobie, you don't have to look hard. Frank Leahy will do. The man who resigned the Notre Dame head post following the 1953 season after a sensational run didn't descend into the depths of gloom that characterized the morose Dobie, but, for publication, he generally took a dim view.

"Notre Dame doesn't have it this year," he prefaced each season. "I don't see how my lads can get by without losing at least three games."

Somehow you felt that Frank really expected to win them all, despite his indignant denials.

Shortly after World War II, a reporter caught Leahy in a mellow mood. This was about the time that Creighton Miller, a superb halfback, one whom Leahy now rates as his all-time best at Notre Dame, was waiting to be released from the Great Lakes Naval Training Station.

"Miller's the finest all-around back I ever saw," Frank confided. "With him on the squad, we couldn't lose."

The reporter returned to his paper with a lot of glowing quotes, but saved them until he saw a small story in a South Bend newspaper announcing that Miller was back on the Irish campus. The next day the reporter ran a banner-line story in which Leahy praised the gifted Miller. Frank tore into a rage when he read the dispatch. In no time at all he had the journalist on the phone.

"What do you mean putting those words in my mouth about Miller?" the Master demanded. "The guy's just an ordinary halfback!"

How much did football figure in Leahy's life? Well, maybe this anecdote Tim Cohane related will give you an idea:

In the fall of 1953, Frank's wife, Floss, fractured her leg running up the stairs in the Leahy home. It was the second day of pre-season practice.

"Gee, honey, I'm awfully sorry," sympathized the Notre Dame coach.

"Frank," the missus said, "it could be a lot worse."

"What do you mean?" he asked.

"Frank," she said, "suppose it had been Johnny Lattner?"

Almost the exact opposite of the gimlet-eyed Dobie and the priestly Leahy was Knute Rockne, one of my favorite subjects. The gnomelike Norwegian put Notre Dame on the football map. Gloomy Gil was suffering lean years just as Knute and his famed Four Horsemen were reaching the peak.

Unlike Dobie, Rockne built egos up. He was a natural salesman, an inspirational zealot. He was absolutely terrific as an after-dinner speaker. Rock, however, added a new twist to pre-game pep talks in 1924. Notre Dame was playing at Princeton and Knute, ailing with phlebitis, was pushed into the locker room in a wheel chair. He didn't feel up to making a fight talk. Luckily, the Notre Dame dressing room was right next to Princeton's.

Just as Rockne opened his mouth to speak, the raucous tones of Bill Roper, the dynamic Princeton coach, began drifting through the flimsy doors that separated the Irish from the Tigers.

Rockne winked at his four scourges, Elmer Layden, Don Miller, Harry Stuhldreher and Jimmy Crowley.

"They tell me that this Roper is a terrific orator," he said, turning to the rest of the team. "You fellas just lay on the floor and listen to him while I save my voice. Maybe you'll learn something."

Pinned down, Rockne admitted one time that his undefeated 1929-30 Notre Dame teams were perhaps his strongest.

"They packed more sheer power than the Four Horsemen team," Rock said. He added that the 1930 creation was, in his opinion, the all-time champs. This was the squad, you'll recall, that had Marchie Schwartz, Joe Savoldi, Martie Brill and Frank Carideo in the backfield. Carideo quarterbacked that bunch and played virtually every second of every game. The second-string quarterback seldom got in a game.

Rockne, who had a habit of giving his players impromptu quizzes, collared Carideo's substitute in practice one afternoon. "It's our ball on the enemy's two-yard line, fourth down, goal to go," he barked to the unsung quarterback. "What would you do?"

"Move over on the bench a little so I could see the touchdown better," replied the sub.

George Gipp, idol of Notre Dame men, was Rock's favorite football player. Knute wouldn't admit it, but he relaxed the rules of discipline for the Gipper. And Gipp had a weakness for gambling and smoking. He was a wizard at cards and pool and would hang around the South Bend pool parlors and beat the sure-thing boys by sheer brilliance. He gave the money he won to needy families in the slum section of South Bend, a veritable Robin Hood. Small wonder the townfolk loved him! Nobody could help loving his gallant, carefree genius. Rock just winked at Gipp's transgressions.

"How's the asthma today, Gipper?" Rock would ask when his ace appeared sluggish in practice after being out late the night before.

Gipp cut practice whenever possible—it bored him— but he ran wild through Notre Dame's opponents. I'd rate him the most versatile back of all time. Minnesota stopped Red Grange by having its ends hold their stations and turn him inside, but nobody ever stopped Gipp. And how he could pass and kick! His flair for gambling was evident in his daring football generalship. He always did the unexpected.

Gipp virtually gave his life for Notre Dame on the playing field, contracting a fatal illness from exposure in the 1920 Northwestern game. He got off a sickbed to make the trip to Evanston. An icy wind cut across the field, chilling Gipp to the marrow. He died of pneumonia a fortnight later. Just before the end came, Father Haggerty baptized him in the Catholic faith.

As far as training rules went, Coach Stagg was a total abstainer and a crusader against smoking. I'm afraid Gipp, as great as he was, wouldn't have lasted long playing for Lon. As coach at Chicago, Stagg could smell a cigarette a mile away, and banished one star for keeps when he caught him sneaking a smoke. He made no allowance for the suppressed intense type of natural athlete who simply must let off steam and rebels against training rules. I never drank or smoked myself, and I have always told those boys wanting to make good in football to do likewise.

The late Jim Thorpe, the greatest of pre-World War I backs, was another who ignored training rules. He was a constant headache to Coach Pop Warner. Jim had an Indian's weakness for firewater. Warner will tell you that Ernie Nevers, whom he coached at Stanford, was a greater fullback than Thorpe, because Jim had a lazy streak and shirked practice. But deep in his heart, Pop knew the Indian was the better man. Thorpe was a born line buster, but he preferred to sweep the ends because smacking the center of the line seemed such hard work.

For leg drive I've never seen Thorpe's equal, but Gipp used his interference more shrewdly than Jim. It was thrilling to watch Gipp signaling his blockers as he raced downfield, telling them which tackler to take out and which to pass up.

"The Gipper had mental poise," Rockne would say. That was a favorite Rockne expression. "Men," he'd tell his players, "you've got to have mental poise out there on the field. Don't ever lose it."

And thereby hangs a tale. In 1921, Notre Dame went to Iowa State and lost, 7-6, for what turned out to be their only loss of the year. A couple of the Irish players lived off-campus in an apartment building and as they returned from the trip an irate old Dutchman named Alphonse, janitor of the building, was on hand to greet them.

"What happened?" he demanded. "What beat you?"

"Mental poise," replied one of the players.

"Hah," snapped Alphonse, "I always knew that bum couldn't play football!"

5

Midwest Memories

Perhaps I will get booted right out of the Loyal Sons of Yale Lodge for saying this, but it has always been my contention that over the span of years the Midwest has played better football than any other section of the country.

Football players seem to grow somewhat tougher, stronger and bigger out in the corn belt.

I coached the University of Minnesota line in 1895, and, until 1910, always managed to get out to Minneapolis for at least a couple of weeks to instruct the defense.

When I think of Midwestern football my mind flashes back to Bernie Bierman, builder of champions at Minnesota for years. Coach Bierman coached my kind of football. He stressed sound fundamentals.

"I believe," Bierman said one time, "that fundamentals such as blocking, charging, tackling and ball carrying, to mention only a few, are more important than plays themselves. I favor a calm, determined team rather than one keyed up to a hysterical pitch for a game."

Bierman laid the foundations of great Gopher teams on the theory that his lads could run and could be taught to block.

"If you like to see our ball-carriers trot across the goal line," he told his linemen, "you other men will have to clear the way. Our running game pins its faith on sound, crisp blocking and plenty of it."

When I think of blocking consciousness, I am reminded of Jimmy Coffis, who played right halfback for Stanford twenty years ago. The Indians were up against Southern California in 1935 when one of the plays ended with a Trojan man on the ground, temporarily disabled.

Little Jimmy, much concerned, rushed to the injured man and started massaging his leg vigorously. The fallen gladiator responded in time, took to his feet and tried the leg gingerly. He flashed a smile of thanks at Jimmy and trotted back to his position.

"How come?" Bobby Grayson accosted Jimmy as the latter jogged back to his place.

"Gee," Jimmy said, "I didn't want to see that fellow taken out of the game. He's the easiest guy to block I've ever bumped up against."

Speaking of open-field blocking and tackling, Doc Spears once had a high-stepping halfback at Toledo University.

The halfback took the ball from center on a certain play. He dashed to the right, where a rival tackler took a shot at him and missed, and then reversed his field and darted straight across for the opposite side line.

Over there, the same tackler took another shot at him and missed again. Finding himself blocked, however, the ball-carrier pivoted, started for the first side of the field once more. Over there the persistent tackler missed again. He rolled over on his side and rested his head on his elbow.

"I'm gonna stay here and rest up a bit," he panted. "He'll be back this way again."

That yarn is a variation of the one Coach Lisle Blackbourn of Marquette tells about Al Thomas, a member of his 1952 edition. Marquette was playing Holy Cross and Thomas lunged at a Crusader runner, missed, and lay lifeless as death on the ground. While he was prone, the carrier retraced his steps and Thomas nailed him.

"That was a nice tackle," Coach Blackbourn said later, "but why didn't you get up right away after you missed him the first time?"

"I figured if I stayed there long enough he'd be back," Thomas replied.

All football fundamentals become instinctive to first-string players through constant practice. You see lots of football players come and go through the years, especially now that television brings them into your living room. Some of these are blockers and little more. They couldn't take a ball for a gain if it meant their graduation. Others are blockers and, in addition, everything required to make an all-around star. There was Steve Meilinger, for example. In 1952, the 6-foot-2, 230-pounder carried a weak Kentucky team alone. He played end, blocked brutally, punted, caught passes, backed up the line, played safety. With two days' practice, he took over as split-T quarterback, and beat Miami of Coral Gables and Tulane singlehanded. He was a Grade A illustration of an all-around player.

The next time you watch a football game, study the defensive line play. You'll notice that most of the boys are watching their opponents and not looking at the ball. No wonder they're so slow off the mark!

Why was Bronko Nagurski, Minnesota's 1929 All-American, such a great performer? Because he kept his head up and his eyes on the ball. He reminded me of a wise old mule in a pasture with a bunch of horses. The mule may look dumb, but he sees everything out of the corner of his eye. Nagurski could play any position on a football team up to the hilt. They used him at fullback a lot because of his line-smashing power, but I think he was even greater at tackle. You never caught Bronko down on his knees, with his nose scraping turf. Nagurski was bigger and stronger than I ever was. More important, he knew how to apply his strength. I'd rate him as the greatest of post-World War I players—equally good at fullback or tackle. What an end he would have made, with his speed and crashing power.

Nagurski probably had more leg drive than even Ernie Nevers. It was nothing for Nag to carry three or four tacklers along with him.

One Saturday he exploded across the Indiana goal line with such momentum that he crashed into the concrete wall beyond the end zone. Doc Spears called him to the bench for a rest.

"How's their line?" the Minnesota coach wanted to know.

The fullback, still somewhat punchy from the crash, shook his head.

"Weak at right tackle," Nagurski said, "but that linebacker on the short side is sure built solid!"

Ed (Moose) Krause of Notre Dame had a reputation for being a One Man Gang, "but I had my troubles with Bronko." The 6-foot-4, 250-pound Man Mountain captained the 1934 College All-Stars against the World

Champion Chicago Bears. The All-Stars had a play which called for Krause to block Nagurski. He banged into Bronko but it did no good. Bronko crashed right over him. The same thing happened a second time.

When the All-Stars lined up again, Moose turned to Eggs Manske, the ex-Northwestern end, and said, "Give me a hand with this guy. Two of us will murder him." Manske, who was supposed to block the safety man, agreed.

They double-teamed Nagurski, but Bronko ripped clean through and scored another tackle. Manske got up slowly.

"To hell with that idea," he grunted, turning to Moose, "my job's to get the safety man. Nagurski's your man!"

One of the most colorful characters the coaching profession has ever produced was Fielding Yost, who established Michigan as a national football power back at the turn of the century.

George Trevor chuckled fit to be tied when he would tell about the first time he went out to Ann Arbor to interview the dynamic Hurry-Up.

"As I waited in the anteroom of the field house, which Yost had himself designed, strange thumping sounds came from the great man's office—crashes as though a gang of house movers were hard at work," recalled the late football editor of the old *New York Sun*.

" 'Don't worry,' his pretty secretary assured me, 'that's only Mr. Yost interviewing a newspaperman. I hope you brought your helmet and shoulder pads with you.' "

Nobody escaped unscathed from an interview with Yost. He believed in personal demonstration and loved to

Handsome and hard as nails, Pudge was the apple of football fans' eyes back in the '80's at Yale, went on to play fifty years of football.

Pudge Heffelfinger, about to bowl over No. 25, played nine minutes of a charity game at Minneapolis in 1933 against college all-stars young enough to be his grandsons. Wearing only street clothes, he was nearly 66 at the time.

The great Yale team of 1888 scored 698 points to the enemy's 0. Members of that juggernaut were, back row, l. to r., Amos Alonzo Stagg, Bill Rhodes, George Woodruff, Pudge, Charley Gill, Fred Wallace, Billy Bull. Front row, l. to r., Lee McClung, Bill Wurtenberg, Pa Corbin, and Billy Graves.

Last picture of Pudge ever taken at a social gathering was at a pre-Army-Navy football game dinner at Philadelphia's Racquet Club in 1952. And what a collection of old-time stars he had with him, left to right: Julian S. Myrick, Trinity; Lloyd P. Jordan, Harvard head coach; James L. Mauthe, Penn State; Isaac H. Clothier, Jr., Swarthmore; Bill Hollenback, Penn; Bill Clothier, Harvard; T. Truxton Hare, Penn.; Edgar Allan Poe, Princeton; Pudge; and George Munger, ex-Penn head coach.

ey Haughton started Harvard's long
of sleight-of-hand quarterbacks.

Walter Camp, father of football.

Frank Hinkey, ferocious and
mean-tempered, remains a legend in Yale football history.

Willie Heston was the spark of Hurry-Up Yost's Point-A-Minute 1901 Michigan team.

Bennie Friedman remains one of the game's all-time great quarterbacks.

Tommy Harmon wrote some of the brighter pages in modern Michigan grid history.

An immaculate dresser, nobody loved football more than Hurry-Up Yost.

Fritz Crisler, after much success at Princeton, went on to become Michigan's counterpart of Yost.

Until Glenn Davis came along, Chris Cagle was regarded as the greatest of West Point football runners.

It took a special act of Congress to award Elmer Oliphant a star for his "A." The great all-around athlete won more letters than any other man in Army history.

No team coached by Earl (Red) Blaik is likely to be either over-confident or lacking in self-assurance.

Composing three-fourths of the 1946 Army backfield named by many experts as the greatest of all time were, left to right, Glenn Davis, Arnold Tucker, and Doc Blanchard.

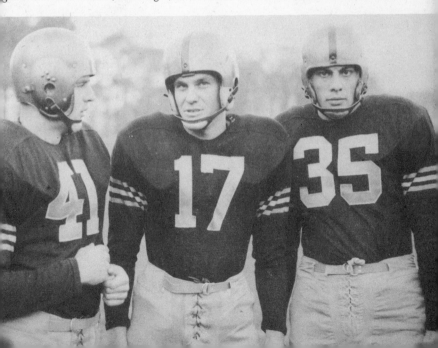

West Coast football fans will never forget, left to right, Tiny Thornhill, Ernie Nevers and Pop Warner of Stanford. Heffelfinger called Pop the most astute of football coaches. The Great Man's trail ran from Cornell to Georgia, back to Cornell, then to Carlisle, Pittsburgh, Stanford and Temple.

Norm Standlee of the '40 Stanford edition was big and fast, could really bowl over tacklers.

Albert was called The Magician while playing quarterback for Stanford in 1940.

Chic Harley's terrific running for Ohio State in 1916, '17 and '19 won him a place in the National Football Hall of Fame.

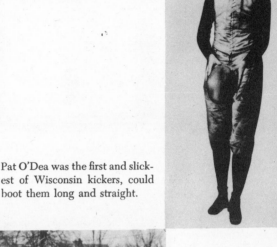

Pat O'Dea was the first and slickest of Wisconsin kickers, could boot them long and straight.

Bo McMillin was an All-American quarterback at Centre College before becoming a stickout coach at Indiana.

THE NATIONAL FOOTBALL FOUNDATION and HALL OF FAME—This organization is composed of energetic, lively men who have known the game long and intimately and have a genuine respect for the good things in football and all it stands for.

What are the objectives of the Foundation? Among other things, to honor the game's immortals, and to make with the scrubbing brushes, with an idea of cleansing the somewhat disorderly house of modern intercollegiate football.

Spade work was actually started in 1947, but it wasn't until the early part of 1954 that the organization's far-flung network of operations became a real part of football's future. Naturally, Rutgers University, New Brunswick, N. J., site of the first intercollegiate game, was chosen as headquarters for the Foundation.

The National Football Foundation and Hall of Fame is in expert hands, captains of industry who have unselfishly volunteered their services. Headed by its President, Admiral John H. (Babe) Brown, Navy's all-time All-American, members of the executive committee include, Chet LaRoche, George Little, Hamilton Fish, Asa

Bushnell, Tom Hamilton, Lou Little, Edwin F. Blair, Col. Edgar Garbisch, Marvin Pierce, J. Robert Rubin, Bob Hall, Joe Hasel, Bill Hollenback, Ed Shea, Bill Cunningham, Joe Sheehan, and Ellery C. Huntington, Jr.

Fifty-three greats were elected to the Hall of Fame, November 1, 1951. In addition to those all-time stars whose time-honored plaques appear in this book, others selected were: Ed Weir, Nebraska; Sammy Baugh, T.C.U.; Benny Friedman, Michigan, Gil Dobie, Washington, Cornell, et al; E. K. Hall, Dartmouth, Dutch Clark, Colorado College; Red Grange, Illinois; Bob Zuppke, Illinois; Hector Cowan, Princeton; Pop Warner, Stanford et al; Ernie Nevers, Stanford; Nile Kinnick, Iowa; Bo McMillin, Centre; Walter Eckersall, Chicago; Eddie Mahan, Harvard; Percy Haughton, Harvard; Fielding Yost, Michigan; Germany Schulz, Michigan; George Wilson, Washington; and Jim Thorpe, Carlisle.

Football has been good to many American men. They have learned lessons in football that have been tremendous aids. The National Football Foundation and Hall of Fame wants others to have this privilege. There is no substitute for intercollegiate, tough, competitive football.

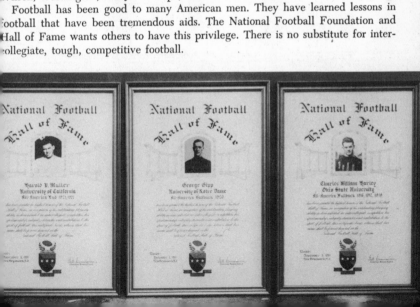

National Football Hall of Fame

Coach Daniel E. McGugin
Vanderbilt University

Coach Henry L. Williams
University of Minnesota

Coach Bennie G. Owen
University of Oklahoma

National Football Hall of Fame

Amos Alonzo Stagg
Yale University
All-America End 1889

Coach Frank W. Thomas
University of Alabama · University of Georgia
University of Chattanooga

Coach Michael J. Donahue
Alabama Polytechnic Institute
Louisiana State University

National Football Hall of Fame

Coach Andrew L. Smith
University of Pennsylvania · Purdue University and
The University of California

Coach Andrew Kerr
University of Pittsburgh · Stanford University
Washington and Jefferson College · Colgate University and
Trenton College

Coach Dana X. Bible
Mississippi College · University of Nebraska
Louisiana State College · University of Texas
Texas A & M College

Herman Hickman, Tennessee's all-time All-American, could take care of one side of an enemy line all by himself.

Brig.-Gen. Bob Neyland developed cision-tooled teams at Tennessee.

Coach Carl Snavely, left, and Charlie Justice, an All-American, gave North Caroli fans much to root about.

Don Hutson of Alabama developed pass-catching to its highest degree.

Dixie Howell, one of the stars that fell on Alabama, ran and passed the Crimson to the Rose Bowl in 1935.

The late Frank Thomas rated his last star, Harry Gilmer, as the finest passer he ever saw.

Few college coaches have matched the late Frank Thomas' record. Six times he took Alabama to Bowl games.

Fritz Pollard ran and passed his way to All-American recognition, led Brown to the first Rose Bowl game in 1916 against Washington State.

Typical of the outstanding players who have come from small-college football was Marv Tommervik, Pacific Lutheran College's two-time Little All-American who established national passing records.

fling the chairs around his office as he illustrated football strategy.

"When the noise gets real loud," the secretary explained to Trevor, "we know he's demonstrating his pet play, Ol' 83."

What followed once George got into Hurry-Up's inner sanctum was a liberal education in the art of football science as the old man expounded his philosophy.

"At Meechigan," he shouted, "we believe that position is more important than possession. We hold our fire till we're fairly deep in enemy territory. Not till then do we spring our scoring plays. Games are lost rather than won. That's why we prefer to let the enemy gamble with passes and trick plays in his own backyard. When they misfire, we seize our opportunity and strike instantly and hard."

Here he grabbed Trevor by the collar and shook him vigorously.

"Why do you suppose we beat physically superior Minnesota teams year after year?" he demanded. "Because we let 'em pile up the first downs while we bided our time and went for touchdowns."

Hurry-Up ignored the critics who called his offense "a punt, a pass, and a prayer."

"Control kicking won many games for Meechigan when we seemed hopelessly outclassed in manpower," he said. "By booting the ball into coffin corner, we kept pressure on our rivals and sooner or later they blundered. An enemy fumble is as good as a fifty-yard run. In Benny Friedman, I had one of the greatest passers and smartest quarterbacks in football history, but I did my share of praying, too. Don't think we couldn't run that ball when we had to. Let me show you how Ol' 83 worked. That was our pay-off goal-line getter, a double reverse with an end around tacked on."

Yost reached for the chairs, and Trevor guessed what was coming. Both the coach and reporter ended up in a tangled heap under a pile of broken lumber.

Meechigan had scored again!

George Little, a truly fine gentleman, was Yost's aide de camp in 1922 and '23, graduated to the helm in '24, before jumping to Wisconsin as football generalissimo in '25. Subsequently, he saw Benny Friedman perform for and against his teams. What manner of quarterback was the shotgun-armed Michigan star?

"Absolutely superb," waxed the man who later became Director of Athletics at Rutgers and now is executive secretary of the National Football Hall of Fame. "Benny threw what I called a 'soft' pass. Any man on the team could handle it. Like Yost said, Friedman, an excellent student, was equally astute, alert and imaginative on the football field. He was a genuine team guy."

Curiously, Coach Little's Michigans were known as the "Comeback Team" in 1924. That's a hot one. The Wolverines were unbeaten in '22 and '23, yet were forced to bounce back and establish themselves as comebackers the next Autumn. How come?

"Red Grange was the culprit," smiled Little. "He virtually wrecked us single-handed. He ripped through us for five touchdowns one afternoon early in the going. Illinois swamped us, 39 to 14. 'Oh, oh,' I said to myself. 'There goes our season.' But, strangely, my kids didn't let down. Friedman wouldn't let 'em. He ran the opposition ragged. We beat Wisconsin, 21-0; Minnesota, 13-0; Northwestern, 27-0; and Ohio State, 16-6."

Little coached Wisconsin in 1925. "I left Ann Arbor a year too early," he said. "I should have waited till Friedman graduated. Wisconsin lost only one game my first season at Madison—and that one to Michigan, 21-0. Or rather to Benny Friedman. Benny figured in all the touchdowns. It was a nightmare. On the very first play he pitched to Bruce Gregory for a touchdown. We kicked off again. On the first scrimmage play, Benny tucked the ball under his arm and skedaddled 65 yards for another score. Later, he passed to still a third TD to complete the bombardment. Like I said, I left Michigan a year too early!"

Antiques think of Hurry-Up Yost as the man who built those unforgettable point-a-minute teams at the turn of the century. Boss Weeks was the quarterback and Willie Heston was the All-American Boy. It was a deadly combination. Heston was a stickout halfback, one of the most amazing runners I have ever seen. In 1902, Willie and his confederates all but demolished Stanford, 49-0, in the Rose Bowl. For years Coach Yost fretted and yowled and bawped because the score was omitted from the Pasadena records. He didn't rest until it was finally added to the archives.

Michigan slaughtered little Buffalo College, 128-0, en route to the Rose Bowl that season. In the third quarter, Yost was amused to find a battered Buffalo player huddled among the Michigan subs on the bench.

"What are you doing here, son?" he asked. "You're on the wrong side."

"No I'm not," the boy said. "I've been in there for forty minutes and I can't take it any more. I'm on the right side now."

One of Yost's old pupils at Michigan, Homer Post, who later went to the Pacific Northwest to become one of the nation's leading high school journalism instructors, recalls the first time he met the Old Man.

"I was an obscure freshman on my way to frosh practice when I bumped into him," Post remembers. "He was dressed in a tall hat, neat suit and was eating peanuts.

" 'What position do you play, kid?' he asked. I told him quarterback.

" 'Quarterback, huh,' he said. 'Come here.' Well, sir, Hurry-Up proceeded to give me the most thorough lesson on how to play quarterback you ever did hear. When he finished he waved me on to the field. It dawned on me later that he hadn't even asked me my name. The fact that I was wearing a Michigan uniform was all that counted with him.

"I never saw a man who loved and lived football more. I once saw him block traffic in the middle of the street while he diagramed a new play with a piece of chalk for Bottle Thompson, the Michigan fullback."

From the fiery Yost to urbane Fritz Crisler is a cycle in Michigan football. Both dramatized themselves while building all-conquering teams. Crisler's spinner-cycle offense was really something to see. It demanded expert execution, matchless timing and flawless faking. Such a complicated attack could not be taught to run-o'-the-mill kids, but, then, Fritz didn't have ordinary material. He had the best his bird dogs could find.

Ironically, Crisler will be remembered longest at Princeton—he coached the unbeatable Tiger teams of 1933 and '35 before moving to Ann Arbor—for the games he lost. That's kee-rect, Yale upset the Princetons of '34 and '36 and Fritz will never forget it.

Perhaps Crisler talked himself out of the 1934 contest, which the great Larry Kelley won on a pass from Roscoe. Fritz got so emotional during his pre-game pep talk in the locker room that the Tigers walked onto the field quivering in every muscle.

"Fellas," cried Crisler, "you have sixty minutes for redemption and a lifetime for regret."

The Princeton players were so worked up that they fumbled seven times in the first quarter.

"I hope the Rose Bowl has handles on it," jested Larry Kelley.

The eleven Yales who started that day were still in there at the finish. Not a substitute was used.

All this reminds me of the afternoon Crisler and I sat with Greasy Neale at Toots Shor's in New York. It goes back to 1945 and Fritz was still coaching Michigan and Neale was the head custodian of the Philadelphia Eagle aviary. "Why do all these modern players fumble so much?" I asked. "In my days the primary requisites for a football player were speed and intellect. And that still goes today, too."

"I wish my boys had more intellect," sighed Greasy. "One day we're having practice in pass defense and one of my backs keeps asking a lineman, 'What time does the train leave tonight? Will there be a diner on it? Is it a large diner?' A great way to learn defense, isn't it?"

"What's wrong with that?" inquired Jack Lavelle, the ponderous Notre Dame scout. "He was merely perfecting his defenses against hunger."

"Hunger?" said Crisler. "Michigan once was kicked out of the Western Conference for refusing to abolish a training table in accordance with Big Ten rules of that era. We stayed out from 1905 to 1917."

Some remarkable broken-field runners have flashed across corn belt football arenas, but the brightest bolt of kinetic energy was Harold (Red) Grange, the Illinois meteor. Picture, if you can, a tall greyhound of a boy, with hair the color of a sunset, the rhythm of a ballet dancer, and two speeds—fast and faster.

Red Grange blazed through Michigan for five touchdowns one afternoon and an irate Ann Arbor zealot scoffed, "All Grange can do is run."

"Yes," retorted Bob Zuppke, the Illini's proud li'l coach, "and all Galli-Curci can do is sing!"

Who can ever forget Grange's first eastern appearance at Pennsylvania's Franklin Field in 1925? The effete easterners had been fed up on the fabulous tales of the Great Redhead's exploits, and they came prepared to be disillusioned. Nobody, they sneered, could be that good!

So what happened? So on the very first play of the game Grange took the ball on his own twenty-four-yard line, slithered off tackle like a gigantic fiddler crab, broke suddenly to the outside, swept the Pennsylvania flank, cut back to midfield, and fled for the goal line. Not a single hand touched him.

Virtually singlehanded Red went on to beat Penn, 24-2, scoring four spectacular touchdowns, all long range.

Grange had what doctors call psychosomatic perception—that is, the ability to sense the presence of unseen hazards. He could visualize the entire pattern of the field at one glance. Even while he was giving one tackler the slip, he could sense the approach of another and was already figuring out ways to elude him.

While there are those who say the Pennsylvania game was his greatest afternoon in football, Grange, himself, told me that his most terrific game was played against mighty Michigan, October 18, 1924. What a performance.

The Illinois players came out on the field without stockings. That just wasn't being done in those days. Ol' Hurry-Up Yost and his Michigan captain, Herb Steger, went over to the Illini and felt everyone's legs. They suspected that they were greased.

"That's one of Zuppke's tricks," said Yost.

Michigan kicked off. Grange took the ball on his five. Following perfect interference, the redhead reached the twenty, the twenty-five, crossed the field, hit the forty, sped past midfield, and kept on going all the way. Not a finger touched him. The Wolverines kicked off again. Once more the ball plumped into Grange's arms. But this time he dropped the ball, recovered, and was tackled. Illinois kicked. Michigan charged down to the twenty-five-yard line, tried a field goal and it was wide. The Illini took over the ball, and on the very first play Grange scored on a seventy-five-yard zig-zag run after coming dangerously near stepping out of bounds at midfield. There was an exchange of punts, and Grange scored again on a fifty-five-yard gallop. A fumble by Steger of Michigan on his own forty-five set the stage for Grange's fourth run to a touchdown three minutes later. Four touchdowns in twelve minutes!

"I got away on another jaunt good for thirty yards, but failed to score," recalled Grange. "It was a hot afternoon and I was so winded from sprinting that I signaled Bob Zuppke to take me out just before the quarter ended. I gained 262 yards in carrying the ball six times. The quarter consumed forty-five minutes because of kick-offs."

Grange was back in there in the third quarter. Right off he skirted Michigan's left end for thirty-seven yards, then carried the ball over from the eleven after passing for twenty. In the fourth period he passed to Marion Leonard for twenty yards and a touchdown. The final score was 39-14. Grange had had himself quite a day.

"I was able to score against Michigan because this was the first game in which I cut back on end runs," Red said. "I ran toward our strong side behind an unbalanced line. In that first quarter the Michigans were thinking more about our bare legs than about the game. Something was wrong with them. We always were expecting them to improve.

"It was indeed a great afternoon for me, but I would have gone nowhere without the splendid blocking by Earl Britton, Wallie MacIllwain, Jim McMillen and the rest. Britton was one of the finest interfering backs who ever lived. Against Michigan that day, I saw him go to the ground taking out one tackler, get up, take out another and finally erase a third before I was downed or clear. Without an Earl Britton there never would have been a Red Grange."

If the Western Conference ever had a counterpart to Grange it was Tommy Harmon. The versatile Michigan halfback, now a successful sports announcer, barely missed Grange's total yardage mark. Harmon was more powerful than Grange, but less elusive.

When Harmon began to take his press notices too seriously, Bob Ingalls, his roommate who played center, went to work on him. Tommy arrived late for practice one afternoon, and Ingalls sang out, "Everybody make a low bow, please, here comes the Michigan football team."

Against Minnesota, Harmon stood back poised like a sculptor's model waiting for Ingalls to snap him the ball. Instead, Ingalls raised up, turned around, and began to grin.

"What's so funny?" asked an annoyed Harmon.

"I was just thinking," said Ingalls, "how foolish you'd look back there if I never snapped you the ball."

Despite his theatrical personality, Harmon could really pick 'em up and lay 'em down once he got his mitts on the ball. He cracked the line like a runaway ten-ton truck coming out of a blind alley and woe to anybody foolish enough to get in his path. Playing tackle for the Wolverines in 1939 was a giant of a guy named Fritz and as he lined up against Northwestern he whispered across to his Wildcat rival, "I don't mind tellin' you, we've just called Harmon's signal over your position. I don't know what you're gonna do, but I'm gonna get the hell outa here!"

6

Dixie Dervishes

It has always seemed to me that Southern ball-car-riers run with reckless abandon, a wild fanaticism that's rarely found in backs from other parts of the nation.

They used to say about Stumpy Thomason of Georgia Tech: "His feet run, his body runs, his arms run, and, by golly, his hair runs, too."

Dixie football history is saturated with such flashy backfield stars as Pooley Hubert, Riley Smith, Harry Gilmer, Johnny Mack Brown and Dixie Howell of Alabama; Ace Parker, George McAfee, Johnny Cox, Eric Tipton and Steve Lach of Duke; Frankie Sinkwich, Charley Trippi and Bull McCrary of Georgia; Ev Strupper, Red Barron, Judy Harlan, Joe Guyon and Stumpy Thomason of Georgia Tech; Alvin Dark, Steve Van Buren and Abe Mickal of Louisiana State; Charley Justice of North Carolina; Beatty Feathers, Bobby Dodd, George Cafego, Buddy Hackman and Buzz McEver of Tennessee; Red Dawson and Billy Banker of Tulane; Doc Morrison and Tom Jenkins of Vanderbilt. There have been others of note, too, but these are some of the greats who come to mind offhand.

While not a few ball-carriers have figured prominently

in Southern football, one lineman stands out above the rest down there like Mount Mitchell dominates the Smokies. He's Herman Hickman, the round guard who played an epic defense for Brig. Gen. Bob Neyland's fine Tennessee teams back in the early 1930's.

Herman wasn't exactly a polished downfield blocker, but he could take care of one side of an enemy line all by himself. He was surprisingly fast for his 250 pounds and he had an agile brain. Herman didn't fool around when there was a job to be done. In 1931, against New York University, he worked over Galahad Grant, a tackle of imposing dimensions. Finally, Chick Meehan, the NYU coach, had to get Grant out of there.

"Tell me, Galahad," said Meehan, "is this Hickman really as good as the papers say?"

"Coach," Grant blurted, "that big guy just called me a Yankee blankety blank and I didn't even answer him back—that's how good he is!"

None of the South's three most famous coaches—Frank Thomas, Bob Neyland and Wallace Wade—were Dixie natives. Neyland was an apostle of power. His tough-fibred Tennessee teams were modeled on the old Army steam-roller principle, which he had absorbed during his cadet days under Pot Graves at West Point. In an earlier chapter we said that the ball is generally in action only twelve minutes of the game. The other forty-eight minutes are spent calling signals, talking things over in the huddle, and otherwise gathering up steam to put the ball in play. So each team is on the move only six minutes.

Neyland learned all this by using a stopwatch and he put the knowledge to work in practice. Before the Alabama game in 1952, he detailed an assistant to sit in the

stands and clock the 'Bama punter going through preliminary exercises. The idea was to record the time it took
the kicker to get off his punts. After ten kicks, the assistant
discovered that half of them were timed in 2.2 seconds
and the other half in 2.3. Neyland, armed with this information, immediately organized a punt-blocking formation which would send a Tennessee man into the
Alabama kicker's path at precisely 2.3 seconds.

"If he takes 2.3 seconds on any kick in the game, he's
a dead duck," declared the General.

Alabama's first kick was 2.3. It was blocked, setting up
a touchdown, and the Volunteers went on to win, 20-0.

Neyland demanded precision and split-second timing
of his horsepower and he generally knew how to get it.

Before illness forced his retirement in 1947, the late
Frank Thomas was hailed as the greatest invention in the
South since Whitney's cotton gin. The Alabama coach's
theories rang with imagination and brilliance. Few men-
tors have matched his record—108 wins, 20 losses and 7
ties (an incredible .841 mark!) in fifteen years at Alabama.
Six times he took the Crimson to Bowl games—three Rose,
one Cotton, one Orange and one Sugar—and only once
did the Tide fail to win.

Thomas was the first Notre Dame graduate to coach at
a major Southern school. It was he who introduced the
famous Rockne system to Dixie. And, despite the passing
parade of football systems, he continued to use the offensive tactics Rock taught him. Thomas never found it
necessary to turn to Yogi, black magic, or the machina-
tions of the tricky T. Year after year, he carried on in the
Rockne tradition, in tactics and results.

"My system was just about the same stuff I was taught years ago at South Bend," Thomas said. "The shifting of the backs and the flexing of the ends were identical. We had four or five basic running plays that were the same and two or three passes that hadn't changed. The only thing we added were reverses and spins to bolster the weak-side attack. All in all, we used only about twenty running plays in 1946. The T-teams had as many as a hundred."

Thomas was a solid coach. He did not believe that a pundit was a magician who could turn mediocrity into greatness with a twist of the pencil, a few mysterious diagrams and a heart-rending story about his sick aunt. He figured that material is worth 60 per cent, with the knowledge of the coach, his ability to impart it to the players, his organization of practice and his personality each appraised at 10 per cent.

"Besides material and coaching, you've got to have your share of luck," he said. "It makes a world-beater out of an ordinary player and a mastermind out of a coach who has made a bad decision."

In 1935, for example, Alabama was playing Stanford in the Rose Bowl. In those days, you couldn't substitute a man in the same quarter in which he was removed, and a player coming into a game had to wait a play before delivering any message from the bench. Thomas sent in a man to tell Riley Smith, his quarterback, not to pass until he was inside the Stanford forty-yard line. Before the sub could legally open his mouth, Smith had called a pass from his own thirty-five, and it was completed from Dixie Howell to Don Hutson for a touchdown.

"I could just hear those people in the stands saying, 'That Thomas, what a genius he is,'" grinned Frank.

Few coaches have done as much with the pass as Thomas did. Frank felt that the receiver was as important as the thrower, even more so on long heaves. It's up to the receiver to use all sorts of guile to get loose. The fancy Don Hutson, who went from Alabama to a banner-line career with the Green Bay Packers, developed pass-catching to its highest degree.

"Although he was astonishingly fast, it was a deceptive speed," said Thomas. "He seemed to shuffle, had no knee action and could drive defenders crazy by feinting and turning on sudden bursts of speed. He never stopped hawking the ball. He was absolutely fearless in making catches. He'd wade right into a pile of men to make a catch and never worried about being hit. He had a sense of timing that enabled him to take the ball at the maximum height of his jump. Don never tightened up. He was as relaxed in the Rose Bowl as he was in practice."

Thomas had wonderful passers during his long tenure at Tuscaloosa, including the great Dixie Howell, who later coached at Idaho, but he rated his last star, Harry Gilmer, as the finest he ever saw.

"And I'm not confining that to Alabama," he said. "I mean anywhere, including the professional game."

Gilmer, later with the Washington Redskins, was a slight, lanky youngster standing six feet and weighing only 157 pounds in college. He had abnormally long fingers, enabling him to get a good grip on the ball, and slick wrist action. In one college game in 1945, he moved to the flank as if to sweep the end and while on the run unloosed a seventy-five-yard aerial downfield!

Thomas, right up to the day he reluctantly quit, had no intention of sacking his beloved Notre Dame system. This despite his colleague's conversion to the high-class T. Why didn't he follow the trend?

"Because," he explained, "in the first place there's nothing new about the T. Notre Dame always had a number of T-formation plays under Rock. We'd come out of the huddle, line up in the regular T and shoot the play from that formation without shifting into the box. Frank Leahy combined both the T and Notre Dame shift at Boston College. In my opinion, you can't combine them successfully over a period of years. You have to use one or the other."

While new plays were added to take care of the ever-changing defense, Thomas maintained that his basic offense was the same that Rockne taught when Frank was a freshman in 1919. Thomas believed the Notre Dame system was better for the passer than the T.

"The ball handler in the T gets the ball, turns and in a flash has to pick out a man to throw to," said Thomas. "It must be done fast. It has to snap. Luckman, Bertelli, Baugh . . . sure, they did it easy. But it's too much to ask of the ordinary passer. We didn't always get Gilmers, you know, but in our Alabama system the passer had a better chance. He had a picture in front of him at all times."

Somebody asked Thomas if he planned to switch to the T in 1945, about the time the mad rush was on to adopt it. "There will be nothing new at Alabama, except new faces," he said. "We're not changing systems. I've spent years working on ours and Rock spent years on it before me. He won—and we've done all right."

No doubt someone once told Frank Thomas never to tamper with success.

Thomas succeeded Wallace Wade at Alabama, who, take it from Mel Hein, produced the greatest college football team of all time—bar none. "I remember the 1931 Rose Bowl in which I played my last game for Washington State," said Hein. "We were up against a pretty fair team that day. In fact, to steal a line from General Stilwell, 'They gave us a hell of a beating.' It was Wallace Wade's last great Alabama team. They whipped us, 24-0. When folks talk about the great teams of the past, they never mention that Alabama team, but for my money they could have licked anybody on that day, including the Notre Dame bunch of the same year that had Carideo, Schwartz and Brill. If you think the T-formation is sca-rewy, you should have played against 'Bama that afternoon. Wade had his men running from punt formation. John (Hurry) Cain, their powerful fullback, would go back there and scrape around with his feet while he barked signals, and you couldn't tell what was going to happen.

"Naturally, Cain didn't get the ball on every pass back, but if there's got to be an original triple threater—well, he was it. He could kick with both feet and pass with both arms. And while you were watching him, one of the 'Bama halfbacks, Flash Suther or Monk Campbell, would like as not tear the headgears off the weak side of the line."

Amen.

7

The Golden Slope

I was sure I had pretty well pushed football out of my mind after graduation from Yale, but a visit from Bill Denman in 1893 changed all that.

Denman was Manager of Athletics at the University of California.

"Heff," he said, "we're still playing Rugby football out on the coast. We'd like you to come out and teach us to play football the way Yale does."

It sounded like a fair challenge and I accepted.

I'll never forget the trip West. I stopped off at Lehigh on the way to Berkeley and coached the football team for a couple of weeks. Then I went to Chicago and joined a civilian All-Star team against Army. We won, but that wasn't the important thing. The important thing was that the game was played under lights—the first night game of any importance played outside under arcs.

En route to the Golden Slope on the last leg of my journey, a passenger sitting across the aisle from me on the train studied me for a moment, then blurted out, "Hey, I know you. You're Jim Corbett. Put up your dukes." Funny, but folks were always taking me for a fist fighter. Another time, on the roof of Blarney Castle, near Cork,

Ireland, a woman walked up to me and said, "I know you, Gus Ruhlen." I don't think I resembled a boxer at all, though I can assure you there was nothing of Ferdinand the Bull about me. Joe Williams once admitted that he always had a secret, sadistic yearning to see me in man-to-man combat with a fellow like Firpo or even Tony Galento.

I wasn't the first Yale man to go West. In 1891, Walter Camp coached Stanford, and Lee McClung served at California. The game between the two rivals ended in a scoreless tie that fall, but I didn't do so well. With Pop Bliss, another Eli, at the Stanford helm, the Indians beat us, 6-0.

(McCallum in for Heffelfinger: Ancients still chuckle about the manner in which Pudge got his Bears in shape for Stanford. He tried to make them as rugged as he was, scrimmaging two hours daily for two months.

One afternoon he organized a practice game, the California varsity against a team composed of Yale and Harvard men and California subs. Heff, of course, got in there himself and played guard for the pick-ups. He opened gaping holes in the center of the varsity line big enough to drive a truck through, and his backs came piling through until they were down on the three-yard line. Somehow, the varsity held and went on the offensive. The first play called for an end sweep. With powerful Wolf Ransome mowing down would-be tacklers, the ball-carrier started wide. Pudge banged through, tried a flying tackle, missed. The runner sped down the sideline, then cut across the field, Ransome still leading the way. There was Pudge waiting for 'em at the five, looking like a mad bull who had lost out on last night's meal. But Ransome didn't see that look. He wanted that touchdown. He hit Pudge squarely in the pit of the stomach. Pudge dropped like a tub of applesauce.

Such groans. "Gee," whispered someone to Ransome, "you kilt him. Now we're really in for it." There the players huddled around, not knowing what to do. And there Pudge lay, writhing in agony, trying to speak. The kids thought he was trying to say, "Git a doctor!" One of the players scrammed after one.

It seemed like an eternity before Pudge could get his breath. Finally it came. The team was ready for a storm, but instead Pudge stammered, "Go-go-good boy, Ransome. Good block." That broke up the meeting.)

Oddly enough, the only three Yale men who became great coaches of the modern game earned their reputations away from home—Alonzo Stagg at Chicago, Harry Williams at Minnesota and Howard Jones at Southern California. All three were originators. What Stagg didn't invent Pop Warner did. It was from Stagg that Jesse Harper learned the Notre Dame system which he passed on to Rockne. Rock was once asked, "Where'd you learn your system?"

"From Stagg," said the Irish coach. "All football comes from Stagg."

Harry Williams was responsible for the Minnesota shift, the daddy of all hike maneuvers. Howard Jones introduced the three-blocker-one-ball-carrier method of backfield play. He had developed fine teams at Syracuse and Iowa before he put Troy on the football map.

Jones was tall and hawk-faced. He hated publicity, was humorless and completely dedicated to his job. Jones had one of the best inside tackle plays ever seen. He built his offense on power plus passing. The tailback, who was the key to his operation, would carry the ball on virtually every play. When one tailback would get tired, in went another triple-threater. Jones called it his "relay system."

Howard's greatest team was the 1931 edition, which beat Bernie Bierman's flashy Tulane Greenies in the '32 Rose Bowl. Blockers don't come any better than Ernie Pinckert and Mallory. Fullback Musick could hit a line like a trip hammer, and Shaver and Mohler gave Jones a pair of versatile backs who could run and throw. If the Trojan attack bogged down, John Baker was there to kick field goals, as he did one year to beat Notre Dame, 16-14.

Howard Jones' Rose Bowl record of five wins and no defeats remains unparalleled.

Far West football hit its peak in the days of Jones. Talk about masterminds. While Howard was giving Southern California the New Look, Andy Smith was doing likewise at California, Pop Warner at Stanford, Lone Star Dietz at Washington State, and Slip Madigan at St. Mary's.

How good were the 1931 Trojans? Well, Georgia had one of its strongest teams that season. Catfish Smith, Spurgeon Chandler (later New York Yankee pitching hero), and Austie Downes were the Georgia stars. They figured to roll over the Men of Troy. Final score: Southern California 60, Georgia 0. The South couldn't believe it. A reception was waiting at the Birmingham railroad depot for the Georgians upon their return from Pasadena. Catfish Smith was first off the train. He started walking down the platform—alone.

"Where are all the football players?" inquired the rooters.

"Out in Los Angeles!" grunted Smith.

Every college has its football legend, and Ernie Nevers is Stanford's. He came from Minnesota and looked like a Viking. They called him the Blond Block Buster because of the way he smacked straight ahead. He did everything well. Not once was he thrown for a loss in two years of college football and a memorable Rose Bowl game. He averaged more than five yards rushing, better than forty-two punting.

Against California, in 1925, his final college game, Ernie, the workhorse, handled the ball on every offensive play but three! He passed swiftly and accurately, kicked long and well-timed punts whenever the Stanford goal line was threatened and got in on every defensive play.

Nevers couldn't play much during his junior year. A broken ankle kept him out of all the important games, but when the Redshirts met unbeaten and untied Notre Dame in the Rose Bowl that season, Nevers was whole again. The Irish won, 27-10, but Ernie picked up more yardage by rushing than the entire Notre Dame backfield.

"Nevers cracked one side of the line for five yards, and the other for six," Sleepy Jim Crowley of the Four Horsemen said later. "We'd pick ourselves off the ground and look to the sideline for help from Rockne, hoping he'd send someone in telling us what we were doing wrong. Nevers drove down to our three. Rock sent in a big sophomore named McMullen. He was so excited at playing in the Rose Bowl before 80,000 people that he completely forgot whose place he was supposed to take.

" 'I'm for Notre Dame,' he told the referee, simply.

"But we were sure he was bringing in valuable information. We held Nevers on the first play, called time and grouped around McMullen to hear the message that would dam the dike.

"'B-b-b-boys,' he stammered and stuttered, 'R-R-Rock s-s-says the trouble is you're not stopping Nevers.'"

Elmer Layden gave an uncanny exhibition of ball-hawking against Stanford. Twice he intercepted enemy passes and ran for touchdowns. On one occasion I saw Layden bat a Stanford pass out of a receiver's arms, grab the ball before it touched the ground, and run fifty yards across the goal.

Rockne relieved his tired star after this amazing play because the game was on ice. Rock noticed tears in Layden's eyes as the boy walked to the bench.

"I know why you're taking me out, coach," Elmer blurted. "You saw it—you saw it!"

"Saw what?" exclaimed the puzzled Rockne. "Have you gone cuckoo?"

"Why," gasped Layden, "I thought you saw me carry the ball in the wrong arm on that touchdown run."

That gives you an idea of Rockne's insistence on detail.

Football greats come and go in the Far West, but few rank with Mel Hein. The old Washington State and New York Giants star was, as Arthur Daley of *The New York Times* once wrote, "the greatest center who ever pulled on a pair of cleats."

When the platoon system was still the passion of the game, a youthful whippersnapper asked Daley, "Would Hein be on the offensive or defensive team if he were playing today?"

It was an intriguing question at that. Hein was a line-backer without a peer. He was so big, so fast and so sure with his hands that few ball-carriers could escape from the bear grip he clamped on them. He was downright great on defense, and he also revolutionized offensive center play. He never made an inaccurate backward flip in fifteen years.

Jimmy Conzelman believed he had Hein when he coached the Providence Steamrollers in the Old National League.

"In 1930," Conzelman told Jimmy Cannon, "I mailed Hein a contract. We expected to get him. He signed the contract and put it in the mailbox but when he got back to his house, there was a contract from the Giants for more dough. He lived in a small community out in Washington State where he knew everybody, including the mailman. So Mel went down to the corner and waited for the letter carrier to make his collections at the box. He talked the letter carrier into giving him the letter back.

"And that's how I lost him. Maybe I would never have quit coaching if I had a guy like Hein. I don't know. But one thing I do know. The Giants would never have had Hein if he wasn't a friend of that letter carrier."

Massive Steve Owen, the large Oklahoman who coached the Giants for so long, is lavish in his praise of Hein. "Mel was the greatest and toughest center ever to set foot on a football field," enthused Stout Steve. "I remember the time a member of the old Cleveland Rams came up to me shortly before Mel retired. 'So that ol' codger's all washed up, eh?' he said. 'Well, I tried to stiff-arm him this afternoon and you know what happened? Ugh! He picked me up and slung me eight yards backward and then sat on my face. What did he do when he was younger—bite their arms off!'"

The modern generation probably casts a majority vote for Eddie LeBaron, College of Pacific's cannoneering quarterback of recent years, as the best little man in Coast football history, but, for my money, Butch Meeker will do. The hard-boiled, cocky midget gave Washington State opponents the slip in 1927. He was All-Coast and even made Walter Camp's All-America second team. I don't think Butch weighed more than 140 and he was as ornery as his nickname implies. Great was his pride when a Washington State wildlife club captured a cougar in the rugged Olympic Peninsula, brought it back to the college as a mascot, and named it Butch, but greater was his disillusionment when some busybody discovered that the catamount was a female.

"Imagine naming a she-cat after me!" thundered the indignant Butch. "If anybody tells the newspapers about this I'll shoot 'em!"

The only way Babe Hollingbery, the Washington State coach, could keep his fiery li'l scatback in line was to threaten to reveal the animal's true identity to the press.

Today the impressive Los Angeles Coliseum symbolizes the power of West Coast football. By the way, did you know that this massive structure was the brain child of reporters Harry Grayson and the late Mark Kelly? That's right. These two upstarts crusaded for big-time football in Los Angeles following World War I, when the only schools playing the American college game in Southern California were Whittier, Occidental and Pomona. Working with Henry Bruce, later Chancellor of the University of Southern California, Grayson and Kelly enlisted the aid of banker Marcus Hellman, who had vast real estate holdings around Los Angeles.

"I'll build a stadium for the city," Hellman promised, "but I want it understood that I want no profit out of this project. It's your job to get the co-operation of the entire press."

From that little acorn grew the splendid stadium which houses the home games of Southern California and the University of California at Los Angeles.

I have met a lot of football writers in my time, but Harry Grayson holds the world's record for phone calls. I never saw a man use a phone so much. Age has calmed him, but back in the Thirties the N.E.A. Sports Editor would call anyone at three o'clock in the morning to ask a question. He didn't care what the subject of an interview thought of him. He was out for the news.

John McCallum, who was Harry's assistant at N.E.A. for three years and traveled around the country with him, recalls one occasion in Detroit when Grayson got into the wrong room in a hotel and called friends in Honolulu, Miami and Mexico City. Another time, before one of Stanford's big games, he called his nephew, Bobby Grayson, an All-American in 1932 and '33, and gave him $230 worth of advice on long distance. It made no particular difference to him that he was phoning from Joe Williams' house.

One night at the St. Francis Hotel in San Francisco, there came a knock on sports writer Henry McLemore's door about three in the morning and Hurricane Harry came bursting in and proceeded to play for McLemore and his wife the entire football game they had seen in the afternoon. Harry played both teams and took time out to be the water boy, too. Then he picked up their phone and called a friend in New York and then a

90 THIS WAS FOOTBALL

friend in Chicago. Then he called a local airport and tried to hire a blimp to take him to Cleveland at once. He left the room in the same whirlwind fashion that swept him in.

Harry, who has never been in a blimp, is probably the most dirigible-minded man since Eckhardt. His recommendation in a time of transportation crisis is:

"Where's a phone? I'll get a gosh darn blimp!"

No story of West Coast football would be complete without a word or two about Lon Stiner, who, along with Babe Hollingbery at Washington State and Jimmy Phelan at Washington, kept the Pacific Northwest in the national football picture.

In 1928 the large, affable fellow rattled West to Oregon State from the University of Colorado with his family in a creaking vehicle. And in Stiner's first season as head coach, his eager Beavers ended a twenty-five game victory streak for national-champion Southern California by holding the Trojans to a scoreless tie—a famous affair in which eleven "iron men" of Oregon State went the entire distance against platoons of Southern California men. The Corvallis unit finished the year briskly by turning back Fordham, 9-6, to the astonishment of all New York.

The Beavers went on winning their share of the upsets for the next two decades under Stiner, including a 20-16 startler over highly favored Duke in the transplanted Rose Bowl at Durham, North Carolina, on January 1, 1942.

Stiner hadn't been in the Northwest long before Jimmy Phelan was warning his brethren: "Watch this guy. He'll come to town like it was farm-market day and make everybody feel sorry for him. Hay shaker, heck! By five o'clock he'll have knocked your socks off."

A Seattle columnist once wrote just before a Washington-Oregon State game: "The Country Cousins from Corvallis are with us again." He went on to imply that the cow-college team from the hinterland with its rustic tutor would shortly be smothered by the Huskies.

Stiner only smiled, and just before the game he sprang the clippings on his milk-fed troops.

"In case you fellows haven't been reading the papers," he said in tones suggesting The Farmer in the Dell, "I'll read an item." The aggrieved Staters rushed forth and zealously belted the big, bad Washingtons all over the field, winning by two touchdowns. After the game, Stiner's still-indignant quarterback handed the ball to the rival captain.

"Here," he snapped, "go plant this—you'll get a swell stand of raspberries!"

Stiner will always be noted for his pregame pep talk the year Oregon State needed only to beat Oregon in the season's finale to clinch the Pacific Coast Conference title. Stiner liked to wind a team tight, especially for his ancient, near-by enemy. But for once he had neglected to prepare a last-minute sock line. In some desperation he finally howled, "C'mon, gang! Let's go get 'em!" Through the dressing-room door he charged, the squad at his heels.

By a stroke of luck, someone had locked the exit to the field. Stiner and his men piled up against it. No key was to be found and the players milled about, cooling off. At this critical moment, Stiner had his supreme inspiration.

Backing up, he uttered an enraged bellow, "Give me room, men! Those so-and-so's can't keep us off of there!" Stiner hurtled his bulk against the heavy door, sending it flying off the hinges. Lon didn't have to say another word. His men went out there and beat the Oregons' ears down.

It isn't generally known, but I did some coaching out in Oregon. I was at California at the time, when an SOS came asking if I would be available to tutor the Portland Multnomah Athletic Club's football team for its game against Stanford on New Year's Day. We had finished the season at Berkeley, so I went up.

I don't remember much about the game, except that Stanford won by a close score. I do recall, however, one rather nutsy play Multnomah had. It had been successful against Pacific Northwest opponents, but the minute I saw it I knew it was cockeyed. In practice, I put on a demonstration to prove my point.

The play was designed to give the ball-carrier triple protection. Running three deep, the interference put their arms on one another's shoulders and plodded through the defense. The ball-carrier also put his hand on the nearest interferer and followed. The idea was for the man with the ball to trail his blockers until he saw daylight in the secondary and then break off on his own for the goal line.

"Nuts!" I shouted. "It won't work against Stanford. They'll bust it up."

To illustrate my argument, I joined the scrub line on the practice field and made the varsity run it against me. Down the field they rumbled. I braced myself. Pow! I

macked into the lead interferer and the whole bunch
umbled over like a row of blocks.

"See what I mean?" I roared. "You're all linked together
and, naturally, if I hit one you're all gonna go down."
They saw my point. The play was tossed out.

8

The Southwest Football's Air Arm

Forward passing has long been the fashion in the Southwest. Youngsters start heaving footballs around as soon as they can swing an arm. It's a spirit that permeates youth like the spirit of Mardi gras in New Orleans on the eve of the Lenten stretch of self-denial.

The Southwest has led the aerial game since the middle twenties when fellows like Mann and Hume of Southern Methodist were hogging the headlines with their needle-point passes. Beyond doubt, the teams in that section of the country have produced the two greatest passers—Sammy Baugh and Davey O'Brien of Texas Christian.

For calm poise, for nonchalance under fire, no college passer has equaled the fabulous Baugh. No matter how many tacklers swarmed on him, Slingin' Sammy managed to stay on his feet until the ball was on its way to the target. Somehow he never lost sight of his intended receiver.

Baugh was once asked which is the more important, the passer or the receiver. "On short tosses," he said, "the passer counts most. A gifted pass-catcher is the main figure on long heaves. More than once, for example, I'd like to have had Don Hutson on the business end of my deep passes."

Baugh played tailback in Dutch Meyer's single-wing attack at Texas Christian. He switched to the T-formation with the Washington Redskins. "It was easier to pass from the single wing than the T," he said. "When you're stationed at tailback you have a better chance to look the field over and spot your receiver. Things happen awful quick in the T slot. Your reflexes have to be much faster."

Baugh had what was perhaps one of the greatest seasons a college player could have in 1936. On a team that had lost most of its stars from the previous year, Sammy was a sensation. In one game he hit the receiver thirty-eight times! Against nine leading opponents, he threw 170 passes, completed 92 for a net gain of 1,100 yards. Eleven of those were for touchdowns. His kicking was excellent, averaging forty-three yards. Baugh ran the team, carried the ball unusually well and was one of the team's defensive stars.

In the fall of 1937, when Sammy was bewildering professional football fans with his shotgun arm, the fathers of Fort Worth didn't tell their children legitimate bed-time stories. Instead, they told the kids how Baugh passed his way downfield two miles during his three seasons in the Southwest Conference. Sam began his football career in his third year of high school. The first pass he ever threw was good for a touchdown. He started as an end.

"But one day I threw some passes," he recollected, "and then I played in the backfield the rest of the season. I went on passing for sixteen years."

During his college career, Baugh pitched 599 passes,

completed 274, netting 3,479 yards and 39 touchdowns. He heaved three winning touchdown passes in each of the games against Baylor, Texas and Rice in 1935.

Speed and accuracy were Baugh's top secrets. "He took almost no time to wind up," Coach Dutch Meyer said. "He shot straight from the shoulder. All action, no loss of motion."

Dr. Wilbur Bohm, the ponderous trainer who looks like everybody's uncle, took care of Slingin' Sam for six seasons and has always been lavish in his praise of him.

"Sam was downright amazing," said the former Washington State trainer who went on to become chief rubber for the Redskins, Washington Senators, St. Louis Cardinals and Cincinnati Reds. "Unlike many star athletes, you seldom saw him around the trainer's quarters. And when he did come in, you could be sure something was seriously wrong with him. Talk about iron men. Why, the week before we played Cleveland for the World Championship—this was at Cleveland, December 16, 1945, and the Rams won, 15-14—one of our players came to me and said Sam was hurting. I went to him. He was in the shower room.

" 'Let me look at you,' I said.

"Sam shrugged. 'Ain't nothin',' he said. 'I'll be okay.'

"Well, sir, closer inspection revealed that he had two ribs torn loose in front. Yet he didn't even bother to come and tell me about it. I taped him up and made him rest and take it easy until the game. I didn't want him to start the game. He had no business out there. But he was as stubborn as a Texas steer and insisted we let him start. He got through the first quarter somehow, but the pain was too much and I made him come out of the game.

" 'Guess you're right, Doc, I'm no good to the team this way.' That's what kind of an athlete he was—always thinking of the team.

"Just because he specialized in passing and kicking and didn't run much with the ball, critics didn't think he could carry the leather. Nuts! He was a terrific runner . . . and equally great on all-around defense. I've seen a lot of remarkable athletes in the thirty years I've been in this business, but Sammy stands in a class by himself as far as modern players go. Only Mel Hein compares with him for durability. I was trainer at Washington State when Hein led the Cougars to the 1931 Rose Bowl, and, take it from me, never once in four years of college ball did he have time taken out for him. He was never on the rubbing table. I didn't even know he was around.

"Yes, sir, when you talk about iron men of the modern generation, you've got to go with Baugh and Hein. The Lord threw the mold away when He made those two."

Contrary to popular fallacy, lightning often strikes twice in the same place, so perhaps it isn't surprising that little Davey O'Brien, 150 pounds of whipcord, followed in Baugh's footsteps at Texas Christian. What is astonishing is that both of these super-duper passers came from Dallas, the town that feuds so bitterly with Fort Worth. Church affiliation accounts for the fact that Baugh and O'Brien picked Texas Christian rather than Southern Methodist.

O'Brien, the Mighty Midget of Southwest football, proved even more spectacular than Baugh. There is always a better story when the little man grabs the headlines. Davey was so short that he had to leap like an Oregon steelhead springing from a trout stream to spot his ends. Despite his watch-charm construction, O'Brien was durable. He missed only fourteen minutes of the 1937 campaign when Texas Christian played a rawhide ten-game schedule.

When Mike Brumbelow, then a high school coach, was first introduced to tiny O'Brien and gigantic I. B. Hale in their frosh year, he said, "That big guy may become the All-America tackle that folks predict, but the little fellow will never get off the bench."

Mike forgot to weigh Davey's heart.

Dutch Meyer, the man who developed Baugh, O'Brien and more recently Danny McKown, always preached the pitching game. He used it as an integral part of his offense, not just a threat when the Fort Worth school lagged behind and had to go for distance. His teams threw from anywhere at any time. But Meyer had been around too long not to know that passing won't work consistently unless it is complemented by a savage ground attack. So he devised what came to be known as the Meyer Spread, and, in 1951, Pacific Coast Conference experts just couldn't believe that a spread would work against Southern California. They were convinced, however, when the Froggies made 436 yards from scrimmage. It also enabled Quarterback McKown to set an individual record for passing against the Trojans, with seventeen completions of twenty-five attempts, for 270 yards. His 340 total-offense yards were the most ever recorded by one athlete against the Los Angeles bunch.

The Meyer Spread became the talk of the sport overnight. Actually, it was nothing new. Baylor, for example, was employing it as far back as 1920. Meyer had been working with it on and off for more than five years before he retired in 1952. Naturally, the main idea was to spread the defense wide and to make more potential holes. It also gave his men better blocking angles.

"Another tremendous factor is that the Spread permits us to get pass receivers downfield quickly, at least four, five on some plays," explained Meyer. "Your pass threat is always terrific, and if you can run just a little, it makes a fine attack. The Spread is a great passing formation, but can be stopped if that's the only threat. You must have a solid running attack to go with it. Some coaches have made the mistake of trying to use it as an adjunct to the T, or something else, and that's wrong. It must be used as the main offensive and it takes a long time to perfect it. A coach can't put the Spread in on Wednesday and expect it to click on Saturday."

Meyer was a highly successful coach because he learned early in the profession that players—and football systems—develop through hard work over a comparatively long period rather than from short intensive drives during the heat of a fall campaign.

Despite what I have said about "the good old days," it is true that the game has become infinitely more exacting and precise than it was twenty-five years ago. Before Brig. Gen. Bob Neyland retired at Tennessee, he had been known to order a certain play to be run in practice five hundred times prior to using it against the enemy. Despite the fiction writers, there is no such thing any more as the flash who drives through for the winning touchdown in the first game he enters. Every lad you see successive Saturdays during the season is the product of weeks and months of rigid, painstaking training. Some boys take until their last year in college to blossom forth and others have reached great heights in professional football some years after graduation.

The football taught by most coaches today has the grace of flexibility and can be attuned to the favored type of play in certain areas, the nature of material at hand, and the foibles and fashions of the day. Yes, there are fashions in football, but I'll bet all coaches are willing to join in prayer that they don't succeed each other as rapidly as in the realm of ladies' fashions.

Bernie Bierman had great undefeated teams at Minnesota in 1934 and '35, but he admitted one time that he would have stressed the forward pass or the lateral instead of the running game if he had been blessed with the kind of material to make it work.

"As a matter of fact," said Bierman, "one season at Tulane I did develop an offense that featured the quick kick, and received wide publicity for my success. I had the boys, though, who could handle that specialty and make it click."

Why does the Southwest favor the forward pass? The weather has a lot to do with it. They play in a warm, dry climate and can count on the air arm more frequently. Northern teams must allow for bad weather and plan their attack accordingly. Teams in the colder climates have done pretty well with the forward pass, however. Andy Kerr developed snappy ball-tossing crews at Colgate, ditto Francis Schmidt at Ohio State. And what about Don Heinrich at the University of Washington? The Husky quarterback set a national record for completions in 1951. Norm Van Brocklin did some pretty fancy pitching at Oregon, too.

The point is this: No team has a monopoly on either

running, kicking or passing. All use the various methods of attack at hand and only serve them up in different combinations. Those stressing the running game merely emphasize it more than do teams with a flashy attack, and vice versa.

Perhaps the first coach to "civilize" Southwest football was stolid Dana X. Bible, who soft-pedaled helter-skelter passing in favor of solid fundamentals at the University of Texas. He stressed line play. Still, when you think of the sagebrush prairie country you invariably think of prodigious passers and phenomenal runners. Fordham still shudders at the mention of Texas A. & M.'s John Kimbrough, and Notre Dame fans will never forget the buffalo-like charges of Kyle Rote of Southern Methodist. Matty Bell, the Mustang coach, pulled a slick one against the Irish in 1949 by switching to a double-wing-back attack, which came straight out of Pop Warner's trunk. Frank Leahy's lads had never played against this formation and were totally befuddled.

Up until this game, Rote played under the shadow of the great Doak Walker, the All-America boy, but an injury sidelined Walker and Kyle got his chance. He sparkled so brightly that afternoon that he even awed his fellow Texans, and Texans never awe easily—they're the "anything you can do I can do better" type! Rote stood out so sharply that he even awed Notre Dame players, and Notre Dame athletes don't awe easily, either. Against the nation's No. 1 team, Kyle ran for 115 yards and passed for 146 more. He scored three touchdowns and his punts averaged forty-eight yards! Kyle was one of those squirmy ball-carriers who didn't go down easily. The tacklers he couldn't jar loose with his hips he made feel as though they had an armful of eels. He thrashed and strained for those extra inches. He was all competitor.

Kimbrough, Walker, Rote, Baugh and O'Brien are typical of the neck-or-nothing kind of backfield operatives that come out of the Southwest, but don't forget Bobby Layne, Koy, Layden and Fields of Texas; Wilson, Mallouf and Mason, Southern Methodist; Brumley, McCauley and Wallace, Rice; Moser, and Conatser, Texas A. & M.; and Grubbs of Texas Christian—just a partial list of Southwest immortals.

While Texans play for keeps, they also have a wonderful sense of humor. By way of illustration, Dayton was playing North Texas in 1952. The Texas fullback bulldozed through the middle of the line. There to meet the rush magnificently was Pat Maloney, fierce-hitting linebacker. The ball-carrier spun as if he had been struck by a freight train. Maloney lay on the sod groggy.

"I didn't know what day it was," Maloney said later. "My folks were in the stands and all I could think of was that I hadda get up. I got up but I didn't know which way to go. I remembered we were wearing blue. The platoons were changing so I just picked out a blue guy and followed him off the field."

"He'd never have made it to the right bench if he'd been color blind," grinned one of the North Texas players.

Texans seem to do things more lavishly. During the platoon era, the standard football bench for a game was equipped with one telephone for communication between the coach and his scouts up in the press box.

The University of Texas had two.

One was for the offensive unit, the other for the defensive forces.

Oklahoma doesn't belong to the Southwest Conference, but geographically it is in with this group. The Sooners have produced some of the nation's finest teams since World War II. Coached by suave Bud Wilkinson, a great Minnesota blocking back, the Okies stress rugged line blocking and downfield interference. You will seldom see a team that cleans out ahead of the ball-carrier so viciously.

After Oklahoma belted Kansas State for its thirty-second consecutive win in the Big Seven a few years ago, a Texan was heard to remark from across the line, "They should win. Their schedule is on the soft side year in and year out. Wilkinson doesn't have to keep his squad up week after week, so has time to rest his players and sharpen them up for the toughies."

The fact is, however, that whenever the superior teams ganged up on Oklahoma, the Sooners managed to do considerably better than all right.

Wilkinson has proven himself a splendid young coach. He has extraordinary home-grown material and is a skillful organizer and split-T man who works at his trade. He is literally a home body. Except when the Sooners are on the road, Bud is never away from the campus more than three hours a week, or when he drives to near-by Oklahoma City for the Monday Quarterback Club luncheon.

Bud Wilkinson's formula essentially is simple. He starts by obtaining remarkable linemen and building matchless lines. Then just about anybody can run in back of them.

A graduate of the Bernie Bierman school, the young man learned long ago that the backs go only as far as the linemen take them.

9

Ivy League Lore

By and large the Ivy League—Harvard, Yale, Princeton, Columbia, Pennsylvania, Cornell, Dartmouth and Brown—lack the football manpower of the state-supported big Midwest schools, the high-pressured Dixie grid foundries, and the powerhouses of the West Coast. But they play spirited, ultra-intelligent football, and the competition is exciting in its own class.

Since the manpower isn't there, the coaching has to be extra smart. For brains, you can't beat the Ivy League coaches.

Occasionally Pennsylvania, Princeton and Cornell will come up with teams that can match the rest of the country. What about Charley Caldwell's 1950 Princetons? That bunch, led by slender, frail-looking, pink-cheeked Dick Kazmaier, was a pippin. I don't think I've seen many more versatile tailbacks than Kaz.

Coach Caldwell's buck-lateral version of the single-wing attack was tailor-made for Kazmaier. The defense was constantly bottled up and kept off balance. Herman Hickman planned a shuttling defense to stop it in '50.

After the kick-off, the Yale coach told Chuck Masters,

his defensive quarterback, "Give 'em 79, where we loop to the inside."

Kazmaier promptly swept around the flank for a Tiger touchdown. "What'll I do next time, coach?" asked Masters, coming over to the sideline.

"Try 78, where our defense spreads to the outside," said Herman. Davidson, the Princeton fullback, rammed through the center for another Nassau score.

"What now?" inquired Masters.

"Only one thing left," said Hickman. "Sit down here and repeat after me—'Our Father, which art in Heaven . . .'"

A good many games have been played on the Yale campus since Walter Camp, player, coach, tactician, rule-maker and well known to later generations as the selector of the All-America team, entered New Haven as a town boy in 1876. More than any other man, he fashioned it into the framework on which the game of today is built and the men he taught at Yale went out to teach all over the country. To illustrate the influence his works and his memory still exert on the campus, Tim Cohane, in his *The Yale Football Story*, relates:

"On a rainy April night, Herman Hickman sat with a couple of friends in the second-floor lounge of Ray Tompkins House. The rain patted gently against the window casements. A lonely limb of a tree scraped beckoningly across the glass.

" 'Be quiet, Walter,' Herman said. 'Go away and let me be. We'll win a few, Walter. We'll win a few.' "

Earlier in this book we told how conveying information via substitutes is generally accepted. It has led to some humorous situations in the Ivy League. One coach had to send in three subs before he could get his quarterback to spring a delayed spinner. Kids can have minds of their own.

Sometimes a quarterback tries to read his coach's mind, with unhappy results. In the closing moments of the 1936 Yale-Dartmouth game, for example, the Elis, trailing by the crap-game score of 7 to 11, had the ball on the Green's two-yard line. To "stop the clock" and prevent time running out, Coach Pond sent in Al Hessberg.

The mere sight of Hessberg—who wasn't allowed to speak to his mates until one play had been run off—suggested K.F. 79 to Humphrey, the Yale quarterback. Hessberg, you see, had been associated all year with this weak-side reverse. Unhappily for Humphrey's hunch, the Dartmouth boys also identified Hessberg with this play, and promptly smeared him. It later developed that Coach Pond had simply singled out Hessberg at random, with no ulterior motive. Ducky wanted a pass, not K. F. 79—ineffective at close range.

To get a bit personal again, in my sophomore year at Yale we lost only to Princeton. We played the Tigers at Berkeley Oval on a rain-swept field. The mud didn't stop Snake Ames from slithering around our flanks. Ames was an Albie Booth type of runner, clever at spinning, changing direction and faking the tackler. It was fatal to go for his knees or legs. They wouldn't be there. We usually stopped Snake by tackling him high.

History repeats itself. Forty years later, Harvard tacklers stopped Albie Booth dead. Albie ran wild through a great Army team in 1929, when the cadets went lunging for his disappearing legs. Harvard scouts saw Booth's field day. "Go for his neck," they told the Johnnies. Albie spent a wretched afternoon at Cambridge, though on one play he missed giving his pursuers the slip by the thickness of his jersey neckband. Heading for open country, Booth was yanked down from behind by the slack of his sweater, when Bill Ticknor reached out a long arm and said, "Come to papa!" If Albie had worn a tighter jersey, Yale would have won the game.

A ceremonious "unveiling" of Booth that freezing afternoon proved a psychological boomerang. Albie sat muffled up on the bench for one period while the Elis staged a long march.

Rushed in cold for a field-goal attempt, Booth did a disrobing act that would have done credit to Gypsy Rose Lee in the middle of Soldiers Field. First he wriggled out of his hooded windbreaker. Next he peeled off a heavy gray pull-over. Then he removed two layers of sweaters. Finally, he accepted his white helmet from an assistant manager and prepared to do a Frank Merriwell.

You guessed it! Albie kicked the ball into his own line. Harvard then paraded to a touchdown. The Johnnies insisted that this unveiling was an act. Yale partisans claimed that Booth had been wrapped up like a mummy because he was suffering from a sore throat. At any rate, Albie's neck was sore after the game!

In my junior year at Yale we again lost just one game. It was Harvard's turn to beat us. They had never won from us previously under modern scoring rules. We couldn't keep Harvard's Ma Newell from crashing through. Newell weighed only 166 pounds, but he had the drive of a mule and the heart of a lion. They called him "Ma" because he mothered lonely freshmen and stood up for the weaklings. Whoever wrote "the bravest are the tenderest" might have had Newell in mind. He was an amateur naturalist and spent Sunday mornings walking through the woods with freshmen, observing and explaining. Ma Newell was killed by a locomotive a few years later while on a track-walking duty for the Boston & Maine Railroad.

Two long runs that caught us napping, after Newell's plunges, finally spelled defeat. First Jimmy Lee, Harvard's fleet little halfback, scooped up a fumble and raced forty yards around Hartwell's end for a touchdown. When we recovered from this shock, Dudley Dean, the Crimson quarterback, squeezed through a narrow slit at center, stole the ball from Barbour's hands, and dashed fifty yards for the clinching touchdown. This stunt revolutionized secondary-defense tactics. Previously we had played our backs about twenty feet behind the line. Thenceforth we stationed them within six feet of the line.

Yale and Notre Dame football teams have met but once, and it isn't any secret that the Eli are content to let things stand. In 1914, Frank Hinkey was coaxed against his better judgment into unveiling his vaunted Rugby attack. Only the year before the Fighting Irish had startled the nation by upsetting mighty Army, with Gus Dorais pitching to Rockne. This earned Notre Dame a shot at Yale.

Coach Hinkey had planned to save his novel offense for Princeton and Harvard, but the Yale alumni in the Midwest, alarmed at rumors about how tough Notre Dame was, demanded action. "We don't want to get licked by a little cow college," they blazed. "Use your secret weapons." Hinkey did, and Yale won, 28-0. The Irish, powered by an unstoppable fullback named Eichenlaub, tore the Yale line to ribbons and piled up more than 300 yards rushing. But four times Hinkey worked his Rugby tactics for long-range touchdowns as the kids from South Bend groped in vain for the runner.

Hinkey was twenty years ahead of his time. The Notre Dame players had never faced a Rugby-type offense and repeatedly tackled the wrong man. Rockne was disgusted. He blamed Notre Dame's defeat on a collective case of "swelled head" caused by too much newspaper publicity.

"I know what was wrong with you boys today," Rock grunted on the homeward-bound train. "You forgot to bring your scrap books with you. The Yale team didn't know how good you were!"

Hinkey tipped his hand to Harvard scouts that afternoon. The Cantabs discovered that the secret to stopping the Rugby attack was to knock the middle man out of the play. Harvard smothered Yale, 36-0. Hinkey never quite recovered from the shock.

Which of all the great teams that rolled on old Yale Field or in the Bowl, was the greatest? Of course, I'll go along with early powerhouses which I played on like Corbin's and McClung's, but the Yale team that most Old Blues and football men regard as the greatest in the school's long gridiron history is the team of 1923. The Big Blue team was coached by Tad Jones and captained by Bill Mallory. The team included four transfers: Century Milstead from Wabash; Mal Stevens, from Washburn; Lyle Richeson, from Tulane; and Widdy Neale, Greasy's kid brother, who reached New Haven by way of West Virginia and Marietta. Yale had strong freshman teams in 1920 and '21 and by the time the '23 season arrived the varsity was saturated with experience and talent. Milstead and Ted Blair probably were the best pair of tackles the Blue ever knew at one time.

When folks talk about great Yale teams, the 1916 bunch is often referred to. Coach Tad Jones said one time he would have hardly called it that.

"But if you had called it one of the most courageous Yale teams of all time you would have been perfectly correct," he added. It was very evident the '16 team was one of his favorite groups. Perhaps the fact that it was the first college team he ever coached stirred his sentimentality.

The year before Tad took charge the Yales were, if you Old Blues will pardon my frankness, pretty terrible. They were beaten by Virginia, Washington & Jefferson, Colgate, Brown and Harvard. As a matter of truth they were massacred by Harvard. The score was 41-0. They did just beat Lehigh by a point. But the first year Jones was in charge, the Yales beat everybody but Brown, who wound up playing Washington State in the Rose Bowl.

"And I want to tell you here and now," explained Jones, "the fellows didn't lose that one. I lost it for them. We had Brown beaten, 6-0, at the half and I told the kids to take it easy in the second half, to save themselves for Princeton and Harvard, which we were to meet on the following Saturdays. I broke up their concentration and their intensity of spirit. I asked them to let down and they did. It was a costly mistake."

Recalling the episode during a reunion of the '16 team years later, Mac Baldrige, who became a Congressman from Omaha, raised a point of order. "Tad," he said, "if you don't mind my saying so, a fellow by the name of

Fritz Pollard had a lot to do with what you call our let-down that afternoon. All he did was run for three touch-downs. I don't think any of us has laid a hand on that boy yet."

Tad Jones shuddered.

"Please don't mention Pollard," he said. "I can still see him racing across our goal line. I wouldn't be surprised if he wasn't just about the best ball-carrier any of us ever saw."

Princeton football history has run to glorified indi-vidual heroes, such arch opportunists as Alex Moffat, Snake Ames, Tilly Lamar, Arthur Poe, John DeWitt, Sam White, Dick Kazmaier and the like. These stars made a habit of doing the unexpected.

Arthur Poe, for example, stole the ball from a Yale half-back on the Princeton one-yard line and raced ninety-nine yards for the only touchdown of the game. That was in 1898. A year later this same tiny lad kicked a last-sec-ond field goal at New Haven to shade Yale, 11-10. He'd never attempted a drop-kick in his life before!

Brown University has been something of a stepchild among Ivy colleges, but the Bruins have had their big innings. There was that morning at the old Polo Grounds in 1910 when Bill Sprackling tucked in a Carlisle Indian kick-off and lugged it through Pop Warner's Braves for a ninety-yard touchdown. Sprackling matched the great Jim Thorpe run for run and kick for kick that game, keep-ing the gawkers in the old red and yellow wooden stands on edge. Thorpe ran out of steam before Sprackling did. Maybe Injun Jim had had one too many the night before.

Still bright in Brown memory are coach Tuss Mc-Laughry's eleven Iron Men of 1926 who played through an entire major schedule without a single substitution.

They demand good football at the University of Pennsylvania, and the Quakers, with a liberal athletic policy, give it to the alumni. Next to Ohio State, these Sunday-morning quarterbacks are the toughest a coach has to deal with. I doubt if the game has seen a tougher man than the roughhouse Bill Hollenback who carried the ball for Penn in 1908. S'help me, he actually played one game with a slight fracture of the leg and shrugged off such minor injuries as shoulder separations, shin splints and hip bruises. Another stickout back in the early days was Roy Mercer, who outgained Jim Thorpe in a sizzling scoring duel in 1910. My old friend, T. Truxton Hare, will always stand out in my mind as the greatest of Penn linemen.

A decade or so ago, when Penn was at its zenith, Frank Reagan was the key man. He had been sought by just about every major college in the East. It developed that Reagan was recruited for Penn by a Philadelphia Catholic priest, who was simply wild about football. This was at a time, you'll recall, when Jimmy Crowley was assembling his great Fordham powerhouses, and the Ram coach made a valiant effort to get Reagan. Crowley even went to the Philadelphia priest and argued that Reagan should attend a good Catholic institution.

"Don't tell me, Jim," smiled the priest quizzically, "that you're really interested in this boy's religious training?"

"Well, maybe not, Father," said Crowley, "but you certainly should be."

They say the longest run ever seen sprang loose during the Penn-Penn State freshman game at State College, Pennsylvania, a couple of years ago. Penn State scored, then kicked the extra point. Grasping the ball as it dropped into the end zone was a small boy, about as big as thirty cents worth of steak. He was last seen disappearing over the fence.

Nowhere do you get such a sense of brooding tranquility as when walking across the Harvard yard, pronounced "yaad." Other colleges have campuses. Not Harvard, nor Virginia. Down at Charlottesville, the terraced enclosure, laid out by Thomas Jefferson, is known as the "lawn," while at Cambridge the grounds were called the "yaad" long before the Colonists revolted against King George.

It would be difficult for any college to surpass Harvard's all-time backfield, composed of Eddie Mahan, Charley Brickley, Eddie Casey and George Owen, who became even more famous as a hockey star. Tall, long-striding Mahan, and tiny, pony-gaited Casey, both from Natick, Massachusetts, rank with the most elusive broken-field runners of the ages.

"What's your secret to dodging tacklers?" Mahan was once asked.

"I give 'em my leg and then take it away," he said.

Li'l Casey was mild-mannered, a greased pig type of runner. Hero of Harvard's 1919 victory over Yale, his career at Cambridge overlapped the war. They say he came back to college to repeat the touchdown run he was cheated out of by an offside penalty in 1916.

Before the season opened that year, Captain Cupid Black of Yale invited Casey to New Haven and gave him a party at Mory's, that quaint tavern which has been identified with Yale since the old Brick Row era. Black and Casey had been teammates at Exeter.

Black had rehearsed his fellow Elis in a little act for Casey's benefit with the idea of showing Eddie what sort of a hard-boiled gang of cave men wore the Blue. When the waiter inquired—"How will you have your steak, Mr. Callahan?"—it was Tim's cue to growl, "raw and ruddy, please!" When the question was repeated to Captain Black, the redoubtable Cupid sang out, "Bring mine running with gore!" Finally the waiter got around to Casey who was sitting meekly in a corner, his gentle eyes registering awe. Eddie was a swell actor.

"And how will you have your steak, Mr. Casey?" the waiter asked.

"Don't bother to do any carving," said Casey. "Just run that steer in here and I'll take a cut at him as he goes by!"

Nobody tried to kid Casey after that.

Cornell, youngest of the Ivy League schools, has always been known for its string of cracking good running backs—Purcell, Walder, Barrett, Kaw, Pfann, Viviano, Dorset and Miller, to name a few.

It's hard to think of Ithaca without picturing 101 Delaware Avenue, a pleasant brick house halfway up the hill where the head football coach traditionally lives. It was there the meticulous Carl Snavely, later of North Carolina fame, lived. Carl was the first coach to make an intensive study of football motion pictures, and he first set up a projection room in his den at Ithaca. He used to scan those action films by the hour.

"The camera reveals flaws the human eye can't see," he used to explain.

Snavely was a shy, stand-offish individual who shunned reporters, the exact opposite of dashing Ed McKeever, who succeeded Carl. A carnival spirit reigned during

McKeever's two-year stay at Cornell. It was always open house at 101 Delaware Avenue when the McKeevers lived there.

McKeever was the man who coached the ill-fated Notre Dame team in 1944, which was trampled by Army, 59-0, worst defeat in Irish history. The Black Knights scored a number of times on pass interceptions. "Army," remarked Tom Meany afterward, "was dangerous every time Notre Dame had the ball."

McKeever sneaked into a subway to get away from Irish sympathizers after the rout, but he was spotted by one of them anyway.

"Ain't you the fella who coaches Notre Dame?" the guy wanted to know.

McKeever nodded.

"Tell me, coach," the man persisted, "didn't your Irishmen play like a bunch of Protestants this afternoon!"

Columbia, despite its huge student enrollment, has fewer men eligible for football than any other Ivy League school. The Lions suffer also from their location in the heart of the world's largest city. The genius of Lou Little nevertheless manages to bob up with at least one stunning upset annually, such as the 21-20 miracle win over vaunted Army in 1947. That was the day on which Bill Swiacki, the acrobatic end, made his incredible end zone shoestring catch of a looping pass from Gene Rossides. It was a stunt Red Blaik still refuses to believe.

The Morningsiders pulled the daddy of all upsets in 1934 by beating a great Stanford team in the Rose Bowl. It might not have happened, though, if the Stanford tackle, end and wing-back—the defensive triangle—had kept their heads up when Columbia pulled its famous short-side reverse by Al Barabas, from a fake half spinner off tackle. Quarterback Cliff Montgomery half spun and faked the ball to Brominski, then slipped it surreptitiously to Barabas, who screened it behind his hip and dashed around Stanford's sucked-in end for a touchdown.

"Three-card Monty," a field general who never got the full credit he deserved, was such a clever actor that all the Stanford defenders were pulled away from the threatened flank. The old shell game! No con man ever city-slicked a bunch of yokels more neatly than Montgomery fooled those Stanford boys on what Lou Little called old K. F. 79.

Coach Little has a knack for developing phenomenal forward passers. Before Rossides came such sure-shot slingers as Paul Governali, Sid Luckman and Cliff Montgomery. Luckman went on to challenge Sammy Baugh for all-time professional passing honors.

Little is the Beau Brummel of football coaches. He's an immaculate dresser, owns many suits, with ties and accessories to match.

Columbia Lou was born Luigi Picolli at Leominster, Massachusetts, but changed his name when he entered Pennsylvania, much to the happiness of copy readers and typesetters. Deep in this vein, I am reminded of Bruce Pfutzenreuter, crack Colorado quarter-miler of a few years ago. He gave public-address announcers ulcers.

One Spring at the Big Seven track and field meet at Norman, Oklahoma, a radio announcer describing the event couldn't pronounce Pfutzenreuter's name. So as the Colorado star rifled past the grandstand, the announcer shouted, "There goes Bruce Pft!"

Bucolic little Dartmouth, founded as an Indian school,

lies tucked away in the vale of Tempe, near the Connecticut River. From 1884 until 1935, the so-called Yale Bowl
jinx hung heavy over Dartmouth's head. Time and again
the Indians shaped up as the best—on paper—only to be
beaten by some weird break.

The most tragic upset came in 1929 when Dartmouth
led Yale, 12-9, with only minutes to go. The Indians held
the ball deep in Blue territory, and all that Tommy Longnecker had to do was freeze it until time ran out. But
Tommy had a brainstorm. He chose that moment to hurl
a reckless, diagonal pass. The ball landed in the arms of
Hoot Hellis, Yale's hundred-yard dash champion who
had been benched all season with a pulled tendon. Hoot
romped eighty yards for the winning touchdown.

Longnecker died in an automobile accident some years
later, still pouting over that blunder which his classmates
had never let him quite forget.

Dartmouth had to settle for a 14-14 tie with Yale in
1924. But for another quarterback's error, the Indians
should have won. Quixotic Eddie Dooley, a tremendous
passer and kicker, was running the works for the Big
Green that afternoon. His girl friend, dressed in bright
scarlet, was seated behind the west end zone, and Dooley
had been waving at her all during the game. On their last
big scoring opportunity, the Indians pushed to Yale's one-
yard line, with fourth down coming up. In the huddle,
Dooley called for Red Hall, a swift halfback, to run the
ball over tackle.

A gaping hole opened in front of Hall as he reached
for the ball, but Dooley never handed it to him. Hall
rushed across the goal line empty armed. Dooley, at the
last second, decided to keep the ball himself. He spun

into the arms of Win Lovejoy and was smothered. Nobody will ever know whether Dooley had promised his girl a touchdown.

Dartmouth's strongest lineman? Gus Sonnenberg of the 1919 edition. He later became professional wrestling champion. Gus cost the Dartmouth Athletic Association plenty of money by ripping out hotel room radiators from the floor—just one of his playful habits. Together with Wild Bill Cunningham and Cuddy Murphy, Sonnenberg formed the tough triumvirate of post-war football at Hanover, forcing Coach Doc Spears to make two pregame speeches.

Doc would chase his three bad boys out of the locker room, then deliver a sentimental address.

"Men of Dartmouth," he'd begin, "your mothers and sweethearts are looking down on you today . . ." Then Doc would dismiss the rest of the squad and call in his three problem children.

"As for you three bums," he'd roar, "if I catch you loafing out there this afternoon I'll run you clean into the next county!"

The good old days.

10

The Big Game

"Gentlemen," Tad Jones said in the cathedral hush
before the Big Game, "you are about to play football for
Yale against Harvard. Never again will you do anything
so important."

Corny as it may sound, there's a great passel of Old
Blues who feel the old Yale coach was right. The Yale-
Harvard fracas is the Big Game all right, a pairing col-
ored with tradition and legend and drama that stirs the
blood in the most sluggish of veins.

D-Day each year is generally the last week in November. For a lot of incorrigible fans, the season opens and
closes with the traditional Big Game.

East, west, all around the country you have Big
Games: Stanford-California, Tennessee-Kentucky, Ohio
State-Michigan, Tulane-Louisiana State, Oregon-Oregon
State, Lafayette-Lehigh, Wabash-DePauw, Cornell-Penn-
sylvania, Syracuse-Colgate, Texas-Texas A. & M., and, of
course, Army-Navy.

Whether there's a national championship, a Bowl bid
or just plumb honor at stake, Big Games invariably are
classics. While wilting before other teams, a squad can

suddenly become absolutely fearless to rise up and slap down an intrinsically superior enemy.

They were comparing all-conquering Boston College with the Chicago Bears in 1942. When lightly regarded Holy Cross poured it on against the Eagles, 55-12, one radio announcer in another Eastern city couldn't believe it. He refused to put the score on the air.

Anything goes. One year a New Orleans' newspaper headlined: "Tackle Caddo Thielman of LSU Vigorously Denies Biting Ear of Tulane's Chambers."

One of the most dramatic Big Games was the 1926 Garrison finish between Ohio State and Michigan. The Buckeyes jumped off to a ten-point advantage, but the young men from Ann Arbor met the challenge magnificently. Benny Friedman's defeat-cheating heaves to Bennie Oosterbaan plopped the Wolverines down in front, 17-16.

The Yale-Harvard series is the New World's counterpart of England's Oxford-Cambridge rivalry. It brings together America's two greatest universities measured by cultural tradition, academic background and worldwide prestige.

You know what happens when a neighbor horns in on a domestic squabble between man and wife! Well, Harvard and Yale are like that. This is a private battle and alien intruders are quickly snubbed.

No combatant can be more adroit in picking the day to sparkle than when these two schools meet in the Big Game. In 1951, to cite a classic example, Ed Molloy was an obscure nobody picking up splinters on the Yale bench. Finally, flushed up from the junior varsity, his big moment came. Harvard was leading the Elis, 21-14, with time speeding away.

"Molloy," barked Herman Hickman, beckoning the recruit quarterback to his side. "Get in there, son."

"Yes, sir," said the young man, and he galloped onto the field. With the poise of a professional and the coolness of a surgeon, Molloy set about blowing the enemy's brains out with a dazzling display of cannoneering. He completed seven passes in a row, the last one for the touchdown that gave the Bulldog a breath-taking 21-21 tie.

Barbershop strategists have poked a lot of fun at Harvard. Back at the turn of the century, wise guys used to say that you had to be born on Beacon Hill or belong to Porcellian to make the Harvard varsity, except that a few South Boston Irishmen were recruited to do the tackling.

In one of the canvas-jacketed Big Games, Captain Coolidge of the Crimson called his men together when Yale had penetrated to the one-yard line.

"Gentlemen of Harvard," he said, "in this frightful expediency, I really think that you men should be introduced. Mr. Saltonstall, shake hands with Murphy here. And Mr. Bacon, say hello to O'Brien from South Boston."

Reminds you of the platoon football era, doesn't it?

One of the early stars of the Yale-Harvard series was Ted Coy. The marvelous Eli fullback was a hulking figure with a pug nose and a shock of yellow hair like a Gloucester fisher girl. He ran like Kyle Rote, his modern counterpart . . . fast and powerful and unstoppable. Coy spoke in a high-pitched treble that seemed incongruous coming from so big a man.

Coy captained the Yales his senior year and beat Harvard with two field goals in the 1909 match. Ted was a great kidder and no sooner had the ball left his foot on those kicks than he turned to Bill Langford, the referee, and kept up a constant chatter while the ball was in the air.

"Mr. Langford," he asked, "did you ever see a prettier kick than that one? Don't tell me you aren't going to give me a goal?"

Coy had a habit of kicking the ball so high that you couldn't be sure whether or not it crossed the bar inside the uprights. He took four shots at the goal posts that afternoon and Referee Langford gave him credit for two goals, but Coy wasn't happy. He protested to Langford.

"What's biting you, Coy?" snapped Langford. "Here I give you 50 per cent of your field-goal tries and I'm not sure even now whether any of 'em went across. Boy, you're lucky and you don't know it."

That silenced Mr. Coy.

Coy punted on first down consistently that day because an injury prevented him from running with the ball. John Kilpatrick, now president of Madison Square Garden, played left end and soon became exhausted covering those sixty-yard kicks. Finally he turned to huge Ham Andrus, who was playing guard, and asked him to take a turn going down under Coy's punts.

Andrus was a stolid chap who seldom spoke and then only to grunt "be gosh." He looked at Kilpatrick perturbed and blurted, "Be gosh whoever heard of a guard going down under a kick?"

Kilpatrick had a persuasive Irish way with him, however, and Andrus reluctantly agreed to chase the next punt. Ham was fast despite his heft and he got down in time to spill O'Flaherty, the Harvard safety man.

"Great stuff, Ham," cried Kilpatrick. "We've found a new end by accident."

Andrus gave Kilpatrick a withering look. "Be gosh I'm through," Ham grunted. And he was, too!

The 1908 game at New Haven stands out grandly in Harvard memories because Vic Kennard ended a long sequence of Harvard defeats with a horrendous drop-kick. Vic had spent the entire previous summer practicing drop-kicks across an improvised goal rigged up on a farm in Maine. Bob Nourse, the varsity center, worked out with him. Together they hatched a plot.

"If I'm sent in to try a field goal in the Yale game," Kennard said, "snap the ball to me the instant I raise my right toe from the ground. Don't wait for a signal from the quarterback. We'll fool everyone."

Percy Haughton, the fabled Harvard coach, had a profound contempt for field-goal kicking.

"It's a sissy way to score," he'd snort.

But Kennard kept hammering away at his special project, and when Harvard bogged down on the Yale fifteen-yard line, he caught Haughton's eye.

"Let me try it now," Vic begged.

Reluctantly, Percy grunted, "Go ahead."

I can still see Kennard standing like a statue behind the huge Harvard line. The ruse worked exactly as planned. Even the lordly Haughton was taken by surprise when Kennard drop-kicked that goal while both lines were still standing erect, waiting for the signal that never came.

"Several years later," Kennard said, "Ted Coy told me,

'We never knew you'd kicked the ball till we saw it sailing above our heads.' Naturally, Nourse and I felt darned good. Not the least of our boyish elation sprang from having slipped a fast one over on old Eagle Eye himself, Percy Haughton!"

It was Haughton who started Harvard's long line of sleight-of-hand quarterbacks who never carried the ball themselves but slipped it slickly to another back with the polish of a magician. He stumbled on this baffling now-you-see-it-now-you-don't attack quite by accident.

The summer before the '08 Yale game, Haughton was fooling around with his Newfoundland dog on the beach at Nantasket. He noticed that when he faked to throw the ball in one direction, then suddenly tossed it to the opposite side, he tricked his pet into falling for the bluff.

"Humph!" grunted Percy. "If I can fool this blankety blank maybe I can fool those Yale bums!"

From this grew Haughton's hidden ball offense, actually the forerunner of the spinner cycle series, later developed by Hugo Bezdek, Dick Harlow and others.

Charlie Buell, Harvard's bland little quarterback in 1921, was perhaps the best goat-getter in the Crimson-Eli series. He kept up a running patter of jibes in his suave, broad A accents. His patronizing tone and supercilious bearing irritated the Yales and Charlie knew it. He would stand back there with his hands on his hips, smile provocatively at the Elis, and, facing around, inquire politely, "Mr. Owen, will you be good enough to escort the ball through left tackle?"

The 1921 Big Game at Cambridge was rich in humor. Early in the game, referee Tiny Maxwell, built on the ample lines of a coal scow, acted as unwitting interference for Aldrich. The Yale captain used Maxwell as a hitching post on an end run, hiding behind Tiny's massive bulk, and dodging this way and that as Harvard tacklers vainly tried to nab him. Finally, Aldrich broke clear for a twenty-yard gain.

Maxwell, a born wit whose humor was enriched by the fact that he stuttered, covered his embarrassment by blowing his whistle.

"T-T-Time out," he sputtered, "w-w-while I g-g-get my bla-bla-blue jersey!"

Two of the greatest players ever to play for Yale against Harvard were Larry Kelley and Clint Frank of the middle 1930's. Both were All-American in 1936.

Halfback Frank came through with one of the most remarkable recommendations in '36 any football player had ever known. Every coach against whom he played named Frank as the finest all-around back they had faced in years. His own coaching staff placed him on a par for all-around ability with any back in Yale history. Frank was a sure-shot passer at either long or short range. His defensive play was brilliant, his blocking outstanding. As a ball carrier his speed—he was a ten-second man —and power combined to make him a constant threat. His durability was amazing. On the side he called the signals and ran the Yales with unusual smartness.

More disputes and arguments set up around Larry Kelley, Yale's captain in '36, than any single player the game had known in seasons. There were times when his defensive strength was questioned, but the fact that Larry was placed on the opposite side from Frank, on the weaker side of the Yale line, and always given two or three assignments to carry out, indicated he knew what it was all about. Few knew that Kelley's job was to crash through and scatter the interference, leaving someone else to handle the run. In addition, the enemy frequently gave two or three men the job of taking care of Kelley to prevent some of his miraculous catches downfield.

Kelley was one of the most popular football players ever to perform at New Haven. He had a glib Irish wit, stage presence, and the knack of improvising wisecracks on the spur of the moment. His choicest bon mots were mostly directed at Princeton, but after smearing a Harvard sweep in 1934, he tauntingly asked the Crimson quarterback, "What kind of judgment do you call that, Haley, trying Kelley's end on fourth down?"

The laugh was on Larry after Yale had scored its second touchdown that afternoon. He had just made one of his circus cross-over catches in the end zone and was walking out when the referee ran up to get the ball. Instead of handing him the ball, Kelley extended his paw.

"What do you expect me to do," demanded the surprised official, "shake hands with you?"

"I thought you'd like to, sir," said Kelley. "Everyone else does."

11

Man Who Hates to Lose

In my travels around the country I have been asked thousands of questions. One invariably stands out above all the others: Who's the most versatile player of all types of games I have ever known?

Arthur Earle Neale.

Yes, sir, Greasy Neale, the rawboned, leathery hillbilly from Parkersburg, West Virginia, gets my vote.

There was nothing Greasy couldn't do. He was equally at home on the football field or at the card table, on a baseball diamond or basketball court, not forgetting the golf course. He's the only man I know ever associated actively with world-championship baseball and football teams. He played left field for the 1919 Cincinnati Reds and coached the 1948 and '49 Philadelphia Eagles. Moreover, he put tiny Washington & Jefferson into the Rose Bowl in 1922.

In his younger days, he shot regularly in the middle seventies, and once reached the semi-finals of the West Virginia Amateur Golf Championship. As a bridge player, Neale rates up with the Culbertsons, Jacobys and Lightners. *True Magazine* once ran an article on Greasy, calling it, "The Man Who Hates to Lose." That was hitting the nail on the head. He has no patience with dubs and even after being around sports for more than forty-five years he can't take defeat lightly.

Some fifteen years ago, when that childish game called Monopoly had a brief fling, Greasy sat up till four o'clock in the morning fiercely trying to beat Mrs. George Trevor. What a real estate operator he'd have made!

Greasy tried to instill that smoldering spirit in his athletes. He should have been a Professor of Applied Psychology. He once told me, "You gotta get tough with some of these kids. I once said to one of my players between halves, 'You haven't a gut in your body. As soon as you see a Giant or a Bear uniform you curl right up.' He began to cry.

" 'Don't say that, coach,' he begged. And what happened?" Greasy grinned impishly. "He was so mad that he went out and scored seventeen points."

Buff Donelli was standing by as Greasy told the story, and he said, "That's right, Greasy, football players drive a coach crazy sometimes. When I was coaching the Pittsburgh Steelers I was going over defensive assignments before a Redskin game. One of my backs, Art Jones, came to me and asked if he couldn't roam around without a specific assignment, just as he did in college. I told him that such a move would have us playing ten men against eleven. But I foolishly let him try it on the proviso that he watch Dick Todd on long passes. Oh, well, Baugh throws one to Todd and Todd runs right past our Mr. Jones for a touchdown. Since they only beat us 23-21, you can imagine how important that was. Afterward I asked Jones how he let Todd get by.

All-American Nile Kinnick was one of those halfbacks who come along only once in a blue moon. The Iowa star was voted U. S. Athlete of the Year in 1939, has since won a place in the National Football Hall of Fame. A Naval flyer during World War II, Kinnick was shot down and killed in action during 1943.

Butch Meeker was a hard-boiled, cocky little back who gave Washington State opponents the slip in 1927.

Mel Hein, shown as he looked at Washington State in 1930, was a line-backer without a peer.

Lon Stiner built hard-hitting, exciting teams at Oregon State College.

All-America Don Heinrich gave Washington fans something to cheer about in 1952, his needle-point passes setting a national mark for completions.

Football coaches have always been practicing pessimists, but Gloomy Gil Dobie, who gave Washington and Cornell their greatest seasons, was the king of them all.

George Wilson was Washington's All-America Boy in 1925, was elected to the National Football Hall of Fame in 1953.

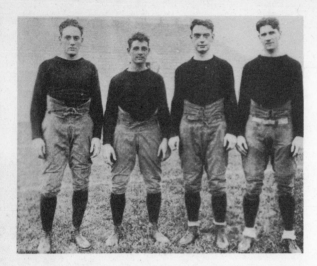

The Four Horsemen, most famous of all backfields. They personified football rhythm. Left to right, Don Miller, Harry Stuhldreher, Jimmy Crowley, Elmer Layden.

The great Notre Dame eleven of 1930. Knute Rockne called this bunch the finest in college football history. The backfield was composed of Marchie Schwartz, Joe Savoldie, Martie Brill and Frank Carideo.

George Gipp, idol of Notre Dame men, was Rockne's favorite football player.

Frank Leahy was a modern counterpart of Gil Dobie, but, despite his pessimism, fans somehow felt that the Notre Dame coach expected to win them all.

The gnomelike Knute Rockne put Notre Dame on the football map. He was a natural salesman, an inspirational zealot.

Bob Zuppke was a fiery coach, and mighty proud of his football record at Illinois.

They called Red Grange the Illinois Meteor. He had two speeds—fast and faster.

Bernie Bierman, builder of champions at Minnesota for years, stressed sound fundamentals.

Bronco Nagurski, the original one-man gang, starred at end, tackle and fullback at Minnesota and later with the Chicago Bears.

Howard Jones of Southern California was humorless and completely dedicated to his job. His Rose Bowl record of five wins and no defeats remains unequaled.

Eddie LeBaron, College of the Pacific's ace quarterback, was one of the slickest and most deceptive ball handlers in the history of the game.

Lynn (Pappy) Waldorf has carried on in the Andy Smith tradition at California, keeping the Golden Bears up among the nation's powerhouses.

...niversity of California football hit its ...ak in the days of Andy Smith. His ...ams were unbeaten from 1920 to ...25.

They still talk about the amazing Brick Muller on the Pacific Coast. He was California's All-America end in 1921 and '22.

Jarring John Kimbrough, All-America at Texas A. & M. in 1939 and '40, charged like a bull moose, was practically unstoppable.

Bud Wilkinson, an outstanding Minnesota blocking back in his day, has proven himself a splendid young coach at Oklahoma.

Speed and accuracy were Sammy Baugh's top secrets. For calm poise, for nonchalance under fire, no college passer has matched the fabulous ex-Texas Christian star.

When Baugh graduated to professional football, All-America Davey O'Brien stepped in and ran the Texas Christian passing attack and became known as the Mighty Midget.

Jim Thorpe was a born line buster. For leg drive, the celebrated Carlisle Indian was in a class all his own.

For all his Biblical precepts, Amos Alonzo Stagg was the foxiest of gridiron tacticians.

Jock Sutherland scaled the football coaching heights at Pittsburgh. He was a strict taskmaster, but was loved and respected by all his players.

lark Shaughnessy is one of the coun- y's soundest coaches. He was one of e first to fully understand and develop e T formation while at Stanford and laryland.

Paul Brown is truly one of modern football's success stories. Jumping directly from Massillon High School to Ohio State and then to the Cleveland Browns, he masterminded victory after victory with teams that featured precision and efficiency.

Dana X. Bible—While other Texas coaches adopted the more spectacular passing game, he continued to more than hold his own with a hard-charging and fundamental approach at Austin.

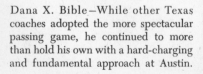

Sid Luckman, one of Columbia's most versatile players, later developed into the first outstanding T quarterback with the great pre-war Chicago Bears.

ou Little year after year starts from ratch and molds formidable teams at always seem to pull the eye- pping upset of the season.

Eddie Dooley of Dartmouth was a tremendous passer and kicker.

T. Truxton Hare was a one-man army in the Penn line. Playing sixty minutes at guard in every game, he made All-America in 1897-98-99-1900.

They played hard, aggressive football in the old days. Few combatants wore helmets. Typical of the ancients was this scene from the 1908 Michigan-Pennsylvania game at Ann Arbor. That's Wild Bill Hollenback breaking through for a big gain—and that's Penn's Harold Gaston throwing a perfect block on the great Germany Schultz, Michigan's all-time All-America center, at right. Penn won, 28-0, was co-National Champion with Harvard in 1908.

" 'I never even saw him, coach,' he said."

Greasy's major-league baseball career suffered from poor eyesight, yet he led the Reds' batters with a .357 average in the '19 World Series. His big-league career was shortened when he crashed into the wall at the Polo Grounds going after a long smash. When he was picked up unconscious, they had to pry the ball loose from his clenched fist!

While Greasy was coaching the University of Virginia football team one year, the baseball coach became sick. The president of the university beckoned Greasy. "Could you help out?" the head man wanted to know. "Is it true that you know something about the game?"

"Who do you think the blankety blank was that played left field with Cincinnati for eleven years?" bluntly retorted Greasy.

He got the job.

About the only sport I ever heard Greasy not caring for was track. Asked why, he said, "I don't give a damn about seeing a kid run unless he has a ball under his arm." A typical Neale reaction.

Greasy's football light was more or less hidden under a bushel at little West Virginia Wesleyan College, but he sparked the first Wesleyan team ever to upset the giant state university at Morgantown. Here's what happened in that one:

In Neale's first varsity game that fall, the team whipped Glenville State Normal with only four plays— an off-tackle plunge, an end run, a lateral pass and a forward pass. Greasy naturally expected the Wesleyan coach to try something extra-special in the way of strategy for the West Virginia game, but the team drilled on nothing but the same four plays they had used the previous week.

"Don't you think, coach, we should try some new plays?" Neale finally asked on a Thursday.

"Bright boy," the coach sneered. "You got anything in mind?" Greasy did. He dug up an old high school play in which the end, tackle and guard pulled out of the line to run interference ahead of the ball. On the spur of the moment, he devised a variation in which a reverse was run from the same play. It caught West Virginia so flat-footed that Wesleyan defeated the state powerhouse, 19-14, for the first time in history.

Greasy, incidentally, was a genuine pro by the time he entered college, largely as a result of having played baseball with Altoona in the old Tri-State League, at $125 a month. But the fact that he was a professional when he entered West Virginia Wesleyan was blandly overlooked in those free-and-easy days. Anyone who mentioned eligibility rules was under grave suspicion of being crazy or a revenue agent. Any good-sized boy who came down the road asking for a game could get one and remain as long as he pleased. John Kellison, for instance, was playing his fifth of eight varsity football seasons when Greasy turned up on the campus in 1912.

Neale's heroics at Wesleyan still are legendary in the West Virginia hills. By 1915 he had so many offers to coach and play that he passed up his senior year at Wesleyan. Time marched on, and, in 1921, he took an ordinary bunch of Washington & Jefferson kids, whipped them together, and produced ten straight wins, upsetting such giants as Pitt, Syracuse, Carnegie Tech and Detroit.

When the little school was invited to meet mighty California in the Rose Bowl, W. & J. authorities hesitated to accept. They couldn't see their team having a ghost of a chance.

"We'd be humiliated," they said.

"Listen," said Greasy, "we may not win, but no team in the world will disgrace us."

West Coast sports writers poured on the razz. "All we know about Washington and Jefferson is that both are dead," they wrote. This drove Greasy and his team wild, and when the W. & J. kids received eighty dollars for pocket money from an alumnus, they went out and bet it on themselves.

Then they held the Golden Bears to a scoreless tie with one of the slickest exhibitions ever seen. California made two first downs and its heralded passing attack, built around Brick Muller, did not complete a single pitch. To this day, Neale swears the officials gypped W. & J. when, early in the game, a thirty-eight-yard touchdown run was called back. At first they said the ball-carrier stepped out of bounds. When they could not find a telltale cleat mark, they decided that Russ Stein, the All-American tackle, had been offside on the play.

"I played football under the two most dissimilar coaches you can possibly imagine," remarked one of Greasy's W. & J. pupils. "Before Neale arrived, we were coached by prissy John Heisman, a meticulous gentleman of the old school.

"'Fellows,' he'd order the linemen, 'lower your rumps!' Then a year later came Neale.

"'Hey, you guys,' Greasy'd roar, 'git them asses down!'"

Despite his disdain for defense, Neale was responsible for originating the five-man line. He pulled the stunt while coaching at Yale in 1937. The Elis happened to have two good centers and only one tackle that season, so Greasy used the two pivotmen as backers-up. The weird formation helped to beat a superior Army team, 15-7.

Neale arrived at New Haven in 1934 under rather strange circumstances. He flatly declares that Mac Farmer, chairman of the Yale athletic board, offered him the head-coach post, a story that, to my knowledge, never has been denied. Between Greasy's verbal acceptance and his arrival in New Haven, however, old grads who insisted on having a Yale man at the helm, had been busy pulling wires behind the scenes. Ducky Pond, an Old Blue, was officially appointed head coach with the understanding that Neale was to be vice-president in charge of strategy and the backfield.

Anybody who recognized Neale's dominant personality might have guessed this arrangement would not work. Jealousy soon crept in. Neale and his charming wife, Genevieve, were never asked to the Sunday coaches' get-together at Pond's home. Furthermore, when Neale diagrammed a new play on the blackboard, assistant coach Stew Scott would jump to his feet and shout, "Wipe that play off, Greasy, you're not a Yale man!"

Little incidents like that constantly popped up to widen the breach. One day Greasy was telling the Yale squad that guys who wanted to act tough on the field had to look the part of it. "I want to see you wear sweat shirts and Levi's on the campus," he was saying. "Above all, I don't want to see any of you guys tricked out in raccoon coats." At that precise moment, Coach Pond walked in—wearing a raccoon coat!

Still Yale managed to win a lot of games. They had smarter, more spirited teams than the Elis had seen for a decade. Newspapers familiar with the situation publicly acknowledged Neale's importance in the picture, which rankled parties who wanted to keep all the credit in the family.

Neale was the only coach Larry Kelley feared. Otherwise, Larry was apt to overlook the rules of discipline. "Jock Sutherland wouldn't have tolerated Kelley on his Pittsburgh team," Greasy said, "but how could you hate a kid who went out and won ball games for you on Saturdays? Half the time Kelley forgot to block—a cardinal sin in Jock's book. Princeton even had a play called the 'Cousin Kelley Special,' designed on the theory that Larry would chase a decoy all the way over to the opposite flank. It usually worked. Yet, when the chips were down, this wild Irishman would come up with the winning play."

Greasy has always said that Kelley had less tension than any other football player he ever saw. Larry would be loose as ashes at the kick-off when most fellows tighten up. His quick thinking under pressure was amazing.

"In the 1935 Harvard-Yale game," backpedaled Neale, "Frank threw a pass which bounced off a Harvard defender's helmet. Kelley had overrun the play, but he calmly retraced his steps and caught the ball casually as it ricocheted off. He never failed to score at least one touchdown in every Harvard and Princeton game during his Yale career. No wonder Kelley's hat size grew so large. You should have seen the fan mail the handsome

Irishman received. Letters came in from gals all over the country, especially from the Southwest. These Janes would give all the lowdown—their size, color of eyes, hair and features. Some offered to lend Larry their sports cars for the weekend.

"'Coach,' he'd say to me, 'let's start a matrimonial agency.'"

Neale, soured by sniping and snobbery, made the last move of his colorful career in 1941 and jumped Yale when Alexis Thompson, a young millionaire sports nut, Class of '36 at Yale, bought the Philadelphia Eagles. Thompson knew that Greasy had been largely responsible for the improvement in the Eli's football fortunes and asked him to do the same for the door-mat Eagles.

George Halas and Clark Shaughnessy, the originators of the modern T formation, had declared that the system could not be put into effective operation in one season. Greasy not only installed the T gimmick in four months, but he made several notable refinements in it.

Greasy had a way with young men. Even the hardened pros played with an almost collegiate fervor for him. He was a great hand at talking a kid into signing a pro contract, but I doubt if he'll ever forget one mission that flopped.

Banks McFadden, a whopping good halfback from the South, had taken an assistant coaching job at Clemson after starring in the National Football League. Neale wanted to bring the boy out of retirement. His telegrams went unanswered. He hopped a train for the land of Dixie.

On the campus they told Greasy that McFadden liked

to spend his off hours lolling under a magnolia tree at a near-by park. Sho' nuff, that's where Greasy found him.

"Son," Greasy said, in an offhand manner, "how'd you like to play for the Eagles?"

The boy yawned.

"Coach," he drawled, "Ah reckon Ah'm mighty well-fixed here."

"But this job's for the birds," Greasy pointed out. "It doesn't pay peanuts." And fishing a contract out of his pocket, added, "We're ready to give $8,000."

"Ah'll be honest with yo-all," McFadden said. "Ah ain't worth no such fancy money. Ah cain't block and, shucks, Ah'm lousy at tacklin'."

"You ain't got much ambition, son," Greasy said.

"No, sir, coach," agreed the boy, "all Ah crave is peace of mind. This is real livin'."

When Greasy took a last backward glance, Banks McFadden was still lying contentedly under the magnolia tree.

Greasy has always felt that you must have a sense of humor to be a good football player. He still uses Larry Kelley as a Grade A illustration. "When Yale was practicing at Gales Ferry in 1936," recalled Neale, "little Charley Ewart was dazed by a jolt on the head. I jogged out and asked the customary question, 'What's your name?'

"Charley winked at me and said, 'Kelley.'

"'Take him out, coach,' jeered Larry, 'the little mug has delusions of grandeur!'"

Neale's slowest-thinking pupil was a fullback named Jack Hinkle. Greasy first met up with the Syracuse lad in Philadelphia. This was during World War II and the players all worked in essential war plants and practiced football at night. Greasy was putting in a new reverse play. Hinkle couldn't get the hang of it. After running through the play a dozen times, Jack still muffed his assignment.

"Gee, son, I feel sorry for your boss at the war plant," Neale said. "You must drive him crazy."

Hinkle was silent for a while.

"Here's a funny thing, coach," Hinkle said later, walking up to Greasy, "they took my boss to the hospital this morning with a nervous breakdown."

Off the field, Steve Owen was one of Greasy's closest friends. On the field, they'd give their eyeteeth to trim the other. Greasy took plenty of kidding from the Giants' coach on his lack of a defense.

"You're so interested in attack," Owen chided, "that your pass defense looks like a Swiss cheese."

Owen is another member of the Old School. Steve was playing with the Kansas City Cowboys back at a time when most coaches today were still in knee pants. I get a kick out of the story Jimmy Conzelman tells about how he missed getting Owen for his Providence Steamrollers.

"We played an exhibition against the Cowboys one time," Conzelman said. "I saw their tackle. He's big, I thought, he's fast. They had a lot of unknown guys from little colleges. They operated that way, paid them perhaps one hundred dollars a month and board. I said to myself I got to get that guy. We made arrangements to buy him from the Cowboys. But I made a mistake. I had asked some of my guys who the big fast fellow was. They told me Kenquist. Milton Kenquist. So I bought Kenquist for $250. I thought I was getting Steve. I didn't know it until Kenquist showed up. Kenquist was a good guard. That's why Steve Owen didn't come to Providence but wound up with the New York Giants. I wonder what would have happened if he hadn't gone to the Giants? We'll never know, will we?"

Neale says the greatest backs he ever coached were Clint Frank and Steve Van Buren. "Steve could hit a shade harder," Greasy said, "but if I had to choose between them I might pick Frank because he was equally strong on defense. Here was a kid who gave it the old college try on every play. When we told him to freeze the ball against Harvard in 1936, with Yale leading, 14-13, and a minute to go, Frank was terrific. He was so groggy that his teammates had to prop him up on his feet after each plunge."

During his college coaching career, Greasy made it a habit to get close to the professors. It helps a lot, he said, to have the faculty on your side when exams are coming up.

"You'd be surprised how many teachers love football," he observed. "I remember Billy Phelps. He was the famous Yale lecturer on the poet, Robert Browning, you know. Anyway, Billy was a hot football fan and treated our players kindly when marks were passed out.

"'Which gives you the greater kick, a perfect recitation in the classroom or a fifty-yard run for a touchdown?' he was once asked by a friend.

"'Well,' Billy said, 'I can't get too excited over a perfect recitation.'"

12

Red Blaik of Army

"Being a football coach's wife is like being married to a doctor," Red Blaik's wife, Merle, once said. "The woman must realize that her husband is wedded to his profession. Next to the Army football team, Red likes me best."

To meet Earl (Red) Blaik is not to know him. And only a few people know the great West Point coach well. One of them is General Douglas MacArthur, who, in the midst of his campaign for the liberation of the Philippines, found time to write Blaik letters during the football season and to send inspiring messages by cable on the eve of the Notre Dame-Army games. Blaik read the exhortations to his players in the dressing room before going onto the field.

Another of the few who know Blaik well is Lieutenant General Robert L. Eichelberger, who, when he was head of the Academy, summoned Red to West Point from Hanover, New Hampshire, in 1941, after Blaik's Dartmouth teams had scaled the Ivy League heights.

"Your alma mater needs you!" Eichelberger wired Red. "Army football has reached an all-time low. Come at once. This is a military order."

138

Duty called and Blaik responded.

The person who knows Red best, of course, is his charming wife, who suffers with him through each football season. Blaik, you know, takes his football with a pain that's almost pleasure. He is not a professional pessimist, but he is inclined to anticipate the worst every autumn Saturday, or at any rate convinces himself that every game is a potential upset.

Blaik communicates this apprehension to his household.

"During the week before the 1945 Army-Pennsylvania game," Merle Blaik recalled, "Earl paced the living room at night and tossed in his sleep when he finally went to bed. Good gracious, he had us all worried. To hear him talk about Savitsky, Penn's 250-pound tackle, and Dickerson, the powerful guard, I didn't think Army had a chance. Earl told us that Evans, Penn's halfback, was the best forward passer in the country. He had me so jittery I broke a couple of dishes in the kitchen. It's like that every week. The team Army plays next is the one Earl fears."

What manner of man is Red Blaik? Well, he's lean of jaw and hard of muscle and, despite his nickname, he's not a redhead at all. His hair is brown, with auburn undertones. A glint of red gleams when the sun strikes at a certain angle. His expressive brown eyes look at you with a frank, level, appraising gaze. His thin lips and firm jaw bespeak purposefulness. His prominent sharply chiseled nose suggests the doer rather than the talker—a man born to command.

Blaik never disparages his own players. Instead, he plays up the other team and points out to his men the job confronting them. Yet no team coached by Red is likely to be either over-confident or lacking in self-assurance.

"Given a team solidly grounded in fundamentals and schooled in strategy," he will tell you, "the issue often hinges on emotional response. A team must be up to win."

Blaik will be remembered best at Darthmouth as "the man who smashed the Yale Bowl jinx." Believe it or not, Dartmouth had never beaten Yale in a series that started in 1886 and continued spasmodically down to 1934, when Red took charge of the Big Green. Time and again, Dartmouth teams which seemed certain winners had been the victims of last-quarter Yale rallies. But his '35 edition scotched the Bowl jinx for keeps.

"What did I tell you?" said Red, as his Dartmouth players trooped into the dressing room after the game. "Those Yale men are just a bunch of kids like you. There's nothing supernatural about a big white Y on a dark blue jersey."

Blaik has never gone in for locker-room oratory before games. There are no fiery harangues, no blood-and-thunder pep talks. He may inject a sentimental note if he senses that it won't strike a false chord.

"The modern youngster is a sophisticated realist," Blaik has always said. "You don't dare work on his emotions with that die for dear old Rutgers stuff. He might laugh in your face. Locker-room pep talks went out of style years ago.

"Before the Pennsylvania and Navy games, cadet players need to be calmed down rather than keyed up. Those games are so hopped up that no fight talk is necessary. Instead, I try to make the boys relax. Football is a game of the mind as well as the emotions. I want my men mentally keen and emotionally relaxed. Otherwise they will tighten up under pressure. You've got to lick overconfidence."

I doubt if Blaik will ever forget the 1940 game between his Dartmouth lads and Cornell. That was the one, you'll recall, in which spunky Red Frissell, one of the most efficient referees of modern times, pulled a horrible boner. With Dartmouth leading, 3-0, Cornell advanced inside the Big Green ten-yard line in the last few seconds of the game. Somehow, Frissell failed to count the second down in a quick Cornell sequence. Even the players on both teams were apparently unaware of this oversight, though motion pictures subsequently showed it plainly. Thus it came about that Cornell had a fifth down, when actually the ball should have gone over to Dartmouth.

In the Cornell backfield was a piperoo of an Irishman named Bill Murphy. A devout Catholic, he murmured a prayer while the Big Red team huddled. "Dear Lord," he said, looking heavenward, "if you let me score a touchdown on this next play I promise to attend Mass every day for a year."

Murphy's plea was granted. At any rate, he grabbed a Cornell pass in the end zone for what apparently was the winning touchdown. After Cornell had kicked the extra point, the game ended. The electric scoreboard flashed the numerals: Cornell 7, Dartmouth 3.

Cornell men went to bed that night thinking they had won, only to tumble out the next morning to hear that they had lost. Blaik had spotted that extra down as he reviewed the movies at a staff conference Saturday night. The pictorial evidence was submitted to Cornell athletic officials, who magnanimously refused to accept an unearned victory. They insisted the score revert to the 3-0 edge which Dartmouth held before the final play. And, if you will check the records, you will note that this is the way it stands in the books. This is the only football game that has ever been reversed as far as anybody knows, and the score reversal could only have been made possible by the fact that this was the last play of the game.

Young Murphy didn't know what to do. He went to his Catholic chaplain at Ithaca and confessed the vow he had silently made in the huddle.

"Father," he asked, "am I obligated to keep the promise?"

The priest weighed the matter.

"My son," he said, "this is an unusual situation. You scored the touchdown all right, but Dartmouth was eventually declared the winner. Under the circumstances, then, I feel you are not required to fulfill that pledge. But this is the first time I ever heard of a football referee double-crossing the Lord."

Blaik will testify that no intercollegiate squad is so pressed for time as his cadets. The Army is restricted to ninety-minute practice sessions. This doesn't leave much time to cram in chalk talks, individual instruction, dummy and live scrimmage and reviewing past games via movies. But during the platoon days he uncovered a way to lick the time element for pictures. He simply erected a tent on the practice field with a built-in projector and screen. Then Red employed the shuttle system. While the offensive platoon was on the field, the defense studied the films and vice versa.

In 1927, Biff Jones headed West Point's football corps

and he brought Blaik in as his assistant. Playing for the Black Knights that year was a redheaded terror from the bayous of Louisiana named Chris Cagle, a regular one-man army. Until Glenn Davis came along later, Cagle ranked in a class all by himself as far as great Army backs were concerned. There are those who think that had he played under Blaik's more advanced play patterns, Chris would have exceeded 'em all.

Cagle's most grandiose play was a wide end run from the tailback spot, terminating in a tremendous diagonal pass to the opposite side of the field. This razzle-dazzle stunt won many games for Army, but it cost the cadets the one they most wanted—the 1929 duel with Notre Dame at Yankee Stadium in sub-freezing weather.

Army was the favorite and right off drove to the Irish thirteen-yard line. On the next play John Murrell was stopped on an off-tackle slant. This was Cagle's cue to spring Army's secret weapon, a fake end run and an oblique pass to his favorite receiver, Carl Messinger. This was a risky play. It opened up the other side of the field to the enemy where Jack Elder, the Notre Dame track star, manned the secondary defense. Elder wasn't too much shakes as a football player, but he could run. He could run the hundred-yard dash under ten seconds, to be precise. Cagle raced like a bloke shot out of a cannon for the right-side boundary, skidded to a stop, and let go that all-or-nothing heave. For a moment it seemed that Messinger would grab the ball on the goal line, but a puff of wind slowed the ball just enough for Elder to snatch it out of the Army end's grasp. The sideline was open to the sprint champion. He went ninety-six yards to score the winning touchdown.

A jinx seemed to pursue Cagle. He was expelled from the Military Academy in his senior year for marrying without obtaining official permission. Somehow Red could never put his soul into pro football. A disillusioned hero, he tried his hand selling life insurance, but that didn't work, either.

Chris was finally killed falling down a subway stairs.

It seemed such an incongruous way for a great athlete to die.

Frank Graham once said, "The next time you hear anybody speaking of great athletes he has seen, ask him if he ever saw Elmer Oliphant. If he says no, you can speak freely—and, if he says yes, you'll both have something to talk about provided, of course, you know about Ollie."

It's hard to think of anyone not knowing, or at least not hearing, of Oliphant. He was one of those super all-around athletes who comes along only once in a blue moon.

Elmer showed up at West Point in 1914 by way of Purdue, where he had already enjoyed three years of varsity competition. Some of his feats at Purdue had been incredible. Although he had suffered a broken ankle in a football game with Illinois, he kicked a field goal to defeat the Illini, 3-0. Knocked down or having fallen in the closing minutes of a basketball game with Wisconsin when Purdue was trailing, 20-21, he shot the winning basket while seated on the floor.

Those were the days of a free-wheeling athletic policy at West Point, and Army football teams were loaded with huskies who had played well and in some cases four years on major college teams. And so, in 1914, no one so much as raised an eyebrow when Oliphant bobbed up at the Point. There he became a legend. Plebes being eligible for the varsity teams, Elmer won four letters each in football, baseball, track and basketball and was heavyweight boxing champion of the Corps.

He was, of course, on Walter Camp's 1916 All-America team, and Knute Rockne placed him on his all-time All-America, linking him with Jim Thorpe and Charley Brickley as the greatest drop-kickers.

There is no need to rehash history, as romantic as lots of football history is, but the year before Oliphant arrived at the Point, a cadet student manager asked to fill in an open date on the 1913 Army schedule, went groping for a midwestern opponent. His eye wandered over the record book and paused when he saw a 1912 score. A school he'd never heard of, Notre Dame, had beaten St. Viator's, 112-7. This was a publicity gimmick that could be exploited.

You know what happened. Knute Rockne and Gus Dorais had spent the summer together as lifeguards and spent every spare moment practicing forward passes. The football world was startled when the unknowns from Indiana upset mighty Army, 35-13. After the game Rockne and Dorais stayed over to teach their technique to the cadets and, by means of the forward pass, Army upset Navy that year.

Today Blaik's Army teams play their home games in pretty Michie Stadium, but it wasn't always like this. Back in the early days, long before Red ever thought of being an officer, the Black Knights played their games on the parade grounds facing Cullum Hall. It was all very informal. No admission was charged. If you couldn't find a seat in the ramshackle circus-type wooden stands, you simply squatted on the grass.

Those were the days when Major Charles Daly, the beady-eyed little martinet who had starred at Harvard, piloted the Army. Daly was a two-fisted fundamentalist. He relied heavily on his line coach, burly Pot Graves, whose credo was brute force and power. Pot was sitting in the officers' club one day when he casually glanced out of the window and spotted a steam roller pounding the road.

"There," he shouted, "is my football team!"

West Point hardly had the manpower to translate Pot's power doctrine into touchdowns in those days, though there were such starbrights as Bunker, Torney, Pullen, Farmer Boy Stacy and King Boyer. There was also frail little Ici Byrne, who seemed miscast as a tackle.

Byrne was the lad who suffered a broken neck under the impact of the dreaded Harvard wedge. They carried him to the hospital where he died later that night. He regained consciousness long enough to ask, "Did we win?"

The chief surgeon lied like an officer and a gentleman. "You stopped 'em, son," he said.

On the wall of Red Blaik's office at West Point hangs a photograph of cadet Ici Byrne. The caption is grim.

"Killed in action," it says.

13

Dream Backfield

From the days of the handle-bar mustache, slick-parted hair, high-buttoned jacket and tall stiff collar, to the modern era of the plastic helmet and nylon pants, football fans have always glorified the backs—and, I suppose, they always will.

If you want to provoke an argument, walk into a gathering and tell 'em which quartet you think was the "Greatest Backfield of All Time."

Would your choice be Southern California's 1931 combination of Shaver, Mohler, Pinckert and Musick? What about Stanford's four magicians of 1940 fame, Albert, Kmetovic, Gallarneau and Standlee? I know that folks in the Midwest would nominate Minnesota's 1934 fierce foursome, Seidel, Lund, Alfonse and Kostka, though Michigan graybeards refuse to admit that the equal of Hurry-Up Yost's 1901 Point-a-Minute quartet of Weeks, Heston, Herrnstein and Snow ever wore cleats.

Easterners will perhaps stand pat on such nifty backfields as Yale's 1909 invincibles (Howe, Philben, Daly and Coy), Harvard's 1913 sleight-of-hand smoothies (Logan, Mahan, Boles and Brickley), Pittsburgh's "dream" backfield of 1937 (Chickerneo, Cassiano, Stebbins and Goldberg), and Boston College's 1940 edition (Toczylowski, O'Rourke, Maznicki and Holovak) which beat Tennessee in the Sugar Bowl.

Super backfields, as you can gather from all this, have been a dime a dozen.

Almost thirty years ago, Grantland Rice first focused the spotlight on the backfield when he wrote, "Outlined against a blue-gray October sky, the Four Horsemen rode again." Of course, he was referring to the great Notre Dame backfield of 1924—Harry Stuhldreher, Jim Crowley, Don Miller and Elmer Layden—perhaps the most famous unit of them all.

This group has never known a superior for smoothly articulated performance. While individually surpassed by other backfields, the Four Horsemen personified football rhythm. They executed Rockne's hike shift with the cadence of the ballet.

But times change. College boys have grown bigger, faster, and smarter. The game has steadily progressed in strategy until now even Notre Dame sentimentalists will reluctantly agree that the Irish have since produced greater backfields than the Four Horsemen. I think I have already pointed out that Rockne himself picked his 1929 backfield—Frank Carideo, Marchie Schwarz, Marty Brill and Joe Savoldi—as his best creation.

Do you know what I think? I think I will have to go along with what Fritz Crisler once told me: "Red Blaik had the best backfield in his wartime teams. In my thirty-odd years of playing and teaching football, I've never before seen two such stars as Blanchard and Davis in one backfield. Illinois had its Red Grange, Michigan had its Tom Harmon, Stanford had its Ernie Nevers, Notre Dame had its George Gipp, but Army had two super ball-carriers. In my book, Blanchard and Davis comprised the finest one-two punch in football history. They whipsawed you to a frazzle. If the defense tightened up to stop Blanchard's bull-like charge, Davis flitted around the flank. If the defense widened to halt Glenn's flank raids, Doc tore your center wide open. It was impossible to rig a defense which could stop the pair simultaneously. Even if you could've checked both, Tucker and McWilliams might have run you out of the ball park."

Red Blaik is a man who seldom lets himself be put on a spot, but even he admitted that Arnold Tucker, Glenn Davis, Tom McWilliams and Doc Blanchard formed the greatest backfield he had ever seen. "Maybe the Chicago Bear professional backfield of 1939, with Osmanski, Luckman, McAfee and Nolting was superior," he confessed, "but I'd still take my cadet combination. I helped coach the flashy Army backfield of 1926, when Cagle, Lighthorse Harry Wilson, Chick Harding and John Murrell ran together. They were good, but this bunch in 1946 had more all-round ability."

Well, let's take a look at the "Greatest Backfield of All Time."

At fullback, naturally, was Felix (Doc) Blanchard. This big guy from Bishopville, South Carolina, stood six-feet, weighed 206 pounds, and he could travel like Man o' War. He was, in fact, clocked for the one hundred yard dash in ten seconds flat. Doc got the pigskin fever early in life. When he was about this high he used to practice place-kicks, while his fourteen-year-old aunt held the ball. A motor truck once bumped into him and knocked him kicking. Doc was soon up and around again, but the truck was never the same. Blanchard celebrated his sixth birthday by smoking a corncob pipe and setting the family barn afire. Fourteen years later he was to set the nation's football fields on fire, but in his first game for Bishopville High School Doc wasn't so hot. He let a Bennettsville halfback run through him for a touchdown.

Doc first attracted the attention of college scouts as fullback at St. Stanislaus Prep, Bay St. Louis, Mississippi. Lucrative offers of board, room and tuition flooded the dark-eyed handsome Carolinian, but his paw, a former Tulane star, picked North Carolina for his son because the Tarheel coach was a relative by marriage. Blanchard Pere, of French-American stock, had played football under an assumed name at Tulane. His parents thought football was too rough and forbade him to risk his neck. Blanchard Senior had no such inhibitions regarding Doc.

The war caught Doc in his freshman year at Chapel Hill. Young Blanchard was an infantry private when West Point talent scouts discovered him in a Southern army camp. "Ideal officer material" was the official verdict. "A helluva football prospect," scribbled the scout in a report to West Point gridiron G.H.Q. Both estimates proved correct.

It wasn't long before they were billing Doc as a second and faster edition of Bronko Nagurski. He was a natural for quick-breaking T-formation plays, in which lightning get-away is essential. Once through the tiny openings made by brush blocks, Doc ran his own interference, trampling over anybody who dared to get in his path.

So much for Mister Inside, as George Trevor once named him. Let's turn to Glenn (Junior) Davis, his accomplice and otherwise known as Mister Outside. At

West Point, Davis stood 5-foot-9, weighed 170, and supplemented Blanchard perfectly, because the Clermont, California, whiz had the dazzling speed to turn an enemy flank. Once Glenn got outside the defensive triangle, he was off to the races.

Davis' nickname was something of a gag at the expense of his twin brother, Ralph, who arrived several minutes earlier. The twins were inseparable. When Army football scouts arranged a United States Military Academy appointment for the athletically precocious Glenn, he refused to accept unless brother Ralph received an appointment, too. This took some fancy doing, but West Pointers have never regretted the extra effort.

At little Bonita High School, Glenn starred in football, baseball, basketball, and track. In his senior year, Davis rolled up 236 points on the gridiron. Big-league baseball scouts admired his throwing arm. "A sure-fire Olympic sprinter," enthused track experts. "A basketball sharpshooter," declared hoop addicts.

Davis made good all these predictions at the Point, though not before descriptive geometry had thrown him for a one-year loss, something enemy tacklers couldn't do.

Glenn was what trainers call a natural. During Plebe year he earned varsity letters in three major sports. He could have added a fourth monogram, had he chosen to go out for track. "Running doesn't interest me," he said, "unless it's linked up with some sort of team game."

Mister Outside's athletic versatility almost posed as big a problem as when Oliphant was dominating the scene. We've told you how many letters Ollie won, but there was no mention about the confusion his fourth letter in each sport caused. No provision had been made for such a symbol.

"My first letter was the 'A' itself," Oliphant said. "The second was indicated by a gold stripe, this one across the middle of the letter. Seems no one ever had won more than three letters and they didn't know what to do about that. Since an Army regulation was involved, they took it up with Congress, believe it or not, and Congress advised sticking a gold star on the letter."

Will wonders ever cease?

Davis smashed the all-time record for the Military Academy physical efficiency test in 1945, racking up 926½ points out of a possible 1,000. Nobody else had ever come near 900 points in this all-round program, which included such agility tests as wall climbing under full marching pack, rope scaling, digging trenches, push-ups, pull-ups, weight lifting, running, jumping, boxing, fencing, bayonet drill and calisthenics.

It is significant that Davis, Blanchard and Tucker finished one-two-three in this competition. What's more, McWilliams, the fourth member of the backfield, broke the record for the West Point obstacle course. The collective performance of this group speaks louder than adjectives, and helps explain why this particular quartet was so terrific on the football field. All four of them were born athletes.

Davis was no Fancy Dan sideline stepper. Unlike many football sprinters, Glenn had the power and grid instinct to knife through needle-eye holes inside tackle. He could dodge or pivot out of a tackler's grasp with a leg drive amazing in a 170-pound halfback.

Now we come to a flaxen-haired, chess-brained lad

who directed the Army T-formation of 1946, who handled the forward passing assignment, and who spotted the soft spots in the enemy defense. His full name is Young Arnold Tucker, a South Carolinian by birth, but a Floridian during his formative years. "Young" was his given name. Tucker stood 5-foot-10 and weighed 170. Notre Dame scouts called him "the perfect T-formation quarterback."

For some reason, Tucker didn't get the publicity he should have. Blaik has always said he was the most underrated player in the nation. In the Army coach's opinion, Tucker had the play-picking judgment of Harry Stuhldreher, who quarterbacked the Notre Dame Four Horsemen, and the limber passing arm of Sammy Baugh, yet sports writers hardly gave Arnold a tumble. Blaik wished he could have kept Tucker's ability a secret from enemy scouts.

On any other team but one that had a Blanchard and a Davis, Tucker would have been billed as a triple-threat star. He could match cross-steps, hep shifts and straight-arms with the best of them in a broken field. At Miami High School, where he piloted the "Stingaroos" to the State title, Tucker was rated the most elusive climax runner ever developed down there. In one interstate school game, he outdid Charley Justice, who later starred at North Carolina. Andy Gustafson tutored the 1946 Army backfield before going to Miami University as head coach, and he said, "Tucker could run like Justice and pass like Alabama's Harry Gilmer, but you'd never know it from reading the papers."

The fourth member of Army's incomparable backfield, of course, was Tom (Shorty) McWilliams. He was a

5-foot-10, 175-pound stick of dynamite from Meridan, Mississippi—further stressing what I have said about the South producing such great runners. Notice that three-fourths of the '46 Army backfield came from Dixie! Anyway, McWilliams lost no time establishing himself as a vital factor in the Point's free-wheeling offense after sizzling for Mississippi State College in 1944. Shorty supplied the comic relief so necessary in the grim military atmosphere which pervades the Academy. He was quickly dubbed The Personality Kid by fellow cadets. He was a colorful character, forever joking in his high-pitched, lazy Ole Miss drawl.

When I think of the keenly-tooled Army backfield, and the splendid way it blended together in those days of the platoon madness, I am reminded of another story.

It seems that the college gridders in 1953 had to learn how to be "whole" players all over again when the limited substitution rule returned. Making a two-way operative is no one-day job. Ron Drzewiecki, for example, could have told you the trouble he had learning how to block. Against Cincinnati, the Marquette halfback threw what he thought was a terrific block.

"How'd you like that block?" he asked his quarterback, returning to the huddle.

"Great," said the signal-caller, "but you were supposed to carry the ball on that last play!"

14

Yea! Yea! Navy

Unlike West Point, which is just a mashie shot from New York City, the United States Naval Academy lies off the beaten path, as the football fan flies. It's a serene, secluded spot on the shores of Chesapeake Bay. Here some of football's brightest history has been written.

There is an easy, casual atmosphere at Annapolis which cannot be found among the grim, gray battlements of West Point. Everything at Crabtown centers around the biggest dormitory in the world, Bancroft Hall. You cannot miss Tecumseh, the fabled bronze statue. It is past this bust of the old Indian chief that the Regiment of Midshipmen parades on the eve of the traditional Army game. Each man slings a penny with his left hand at the old warrior as a gesture of good luck.

They call the Navy boathouse "The Port of Missing Men" because it is there that visiting football writers are entertained lavishly by Annapolis brass. Some of the journalists don't emerge for a week.

Three of the top coaching names in Navy history have been Major Swede Larson, Captain Tom Hamilton and Eddie Erdelatz. All three have had the knack of making boys play over their heads.

Larson, an old Marine Corps hero, had a flare for beating Army. His Navy teams walloped the Pointers three years in a row, from 1939 through 1941, running up a combined total of thirty-eight points to six. Coach Larson, a soft-spoken, fatherly man, did not fit the picture of a fire-and-brimstone Marine officer, but his football teams "put out" like the leathernecks at Saipan. Swede out-foxed Red Blaik in the 1941 meeting between Army and Navy. The cadets scored first, but the middies marched right back to go ahead, 7-6. Then, instead of electing to receive, Blaik ordered the Army to kick off. Navy immediately bulldozed 80 yards in short rushes to clinch the victory.

Coach Blaik took a lot of abuse from Monday-morning Quarterbacks on that one, but, he explained later, in his opinion it has always been more blessed to kick off than to receive.

"I figure it this way," Red said. "If a team is any good defensively, it should hold the enemy inside the twenty-yard line and force a return punt. Thus the side kicking off would get the ball around midfield in position to attack. If your team is not good enough to stop the enemy from marching eighty yards, as Navy did, then it doesn't deserve to win."

Phil Handler, the Chicago Cards' line coach, added still another twist on the subject of defense. He testified that too many teams have the wrong idea about this phase of the game.

"They don't regard it aggressively, as an opportunity to score equal almost to offense," he said. "The running game led the attack in the old days, and it was natural for the defense to hang back. The chances of getting the ball were small. Footballs fill the air today, giving the defense a chance to grab a loose ball and go to the races with it. I say that an alert, charging defense can be developed to be dangerous every moment the other side has the ball. The old idea of defense was too purely defensive. Half the scoring potential was virtually waived. Show the defense how to score and you double the team's scoring threat."

Getting back to Blaik again for just a moment, they tell a gag on him concerning his early coaching days at Dartmouth. Red, it seems, had ordered his Indians to kick off at the opening whistle. Then he raced up to the press-box roof top to get a better look at the formation. Halfway up the steps, he heard a tremendous roar. Reaching the top, he was astounded to see his lads lined up to receive the rival kick-off.

"Didn't I tell you to kick off?" he cried, phoning the bench.

"We did—they scored!" came the glum response.

Tom Hamilton, a beetle-browed operative with the pugnacious jaw of an English bulldog, had been a hard-running halfback on Navy's great 1926 team and he coached the same way, with grim intensity. Tom has since gone on to Pittsburgh as athletic director, but they will never forget him at Annapolis. Perhaps no man has loved football more than this pioneer of the Naval pre-flight training program which salvaged college football during the early days of the Second World War.

It was Hamilton's aim at Pittsburgh to revive the rock-and-sock football which characterized Pitt teams under the late Jock Sutherland. Hamilton's pet football play will probably always be Jock's deep reverse. Jock got so many blockers into action that it looked as though the whole student body had come out of the stands to lead the ball-carrier.

Jock, by the way, was the exact opposite of Hamilton as a coach. He made it a rule never to associate with his players off the field, and he insisted upon being addressed as "Dr. Sutherland." Jock walked on the other side of the street. Nevertheless, his players admired him deeply. He built his teams with the same pains that he took to construct a delicate bit of bridgework in dentistry. And like the dentist that he was, Jock didn't hesitate to use the drill on raw nerves. His attitude seemed to be, "This hurts me more than it does you."

The aloof Scotsman didn't laugh much, but when he did he'd light up like a pinball machine. Back in the middle Thirties he had a student manager named Frank Scott. The same Frank Scott who later became traveling secretary of the New York Yankees, and is now players' agent for major-league stars. Anyway, during a vital game one afternoon, a Pitt star had the breath knocked out of him.

"Get out there with the water!" roared Sutherland.

Scott responded like a guy who had just been stabbed by a fork. He jumped up, grabbed two pails—and tripped over a helmet. All that remained was a damp sponge. Frank took it and squeezed it over the injured player's face. Jock thought that was the funniest sight he'd ever seen and he let Scott keep the managerial job.

Eddie Erdelatz, who took over Navy football in 1950, has something that Larson lacked—personal charm. He radiates a boyish enthusiasm that is contagious. Eddie came, as they say, from the "wrong side of the tracks" in

San Francisco, but despite his tough sandlot background he has a gentle quality that is unusual in a profession as hard-bitten as football coaching. His smile has a warmth that endears him to the player who is being scolded.

Coach Erdelatz rated his one-man task force of '52, Steve Eisenhauer, as one of the best guards he had ever seen in college football. Those who watched the hard-charging All-American fight and hammer rival runners into the sod agreed with the Navy coach. Against Cornell that fall, Eisenhauer made three-fourths of the Sailors' tackles. His name dominated the public-address system. "Eisenhauer made the tackle," echoed the p.a. announcer. And, "Eisenhauer was in on that last play . . ." It became downright monotonous.

"This guy," remarked someone in the press box, "must be sponsored by the National Republican Committee."

When you think of Navy football your mind invariably flashes back to Jack Dalton, who played fullback in 1911 on old Farragut Field which borders the bay. Many a punt by Dalton splashed into the water, requiring the game to be held up momentarily while they fished out the ball.

I doubt if any of Dalton's punts sailed as far as the one by Bob Demoling in 1925. Marquette was playing Navy at Annapolis and the Hilltoppers' quarterback stood on his own twenty-yard line. A strong wind was blowing and Demoling had it to his back. The ball sped to Navy's nineteen, where it bounced once and sailed through the end zone. Before it could be retrieved, it rolled another thirty yards and splashed into Chesapeake Bay. The last anyone saw of it the ball was headed for the high seas.

One ball-carrier who stands out in the memories of

midshipmen is Buzz Borries. His zig-zag running in 1934 carried the ball down a muddy field to within place-kick range of Army's goal. From there, standing in ankle-deep slime, huge Slade Cutter, later a submarine commander, booted the ball between the uprights for an exciting Navy victory.

As the regiment of midshipmen entered Franklin Field in Philadelphia that rainy afternoon, each man dutifully wore his rubbers. The suction from the mud pulled off the overshoes and left a trail of rubbers as they circled the field.

From the Army rooting section came: "Mama says to keep your rubbers on, children, or you'll catch cold."

Place-kicking has figured heavily in Navy wins over Army of the past. Dalton kicked a field goal in 1910 and conquered the cadets, 3-0. He kicked another in 1911 and Navy won again by the same score. The following year there was no Dalton in the Sailors' line-up, but there was a big guard named Babe Brown and he kicked two field goals. Navy won that one, 6-0. This thing must be catching, or do the middies simply have a copyright on field-goal victories? That field goal by Slade Cutter in '34 added up to the only points of the contest, and it was the first time the Navy had beaten the Army in ten years. A young fellow named Bill Ingram stood in the Navy backfield in 1936 and drop-kicked the field goal that beat Notre Dame, 3-0. Fantastic.

Speaking of drop-kickers, one of the best I ever saw was Charley Brickley. The old Harvard star is remembered principally as a kicker, but he was a fine runner, too. At any rate, the thirteen field goals that he booted in 1912 established a varsity record that still stands, and his total of eleven in 1911 remains the next best college mark. Frosty Peters, as a freshman at Montana State, kicked seventeen goals in one game against Billings Polytechnic, but freshmen don't count.

Still, Roy Mills' name is the first that comes to mind in any discussion of kickers. The late Mt. Vernon, New York, lawyer left Princeton to get married and so he never made the varsity, but he spent most of his adult life teaching school kids and college boys how to kick. Without accepting any fee, he tutored punters at Alabama, Duke, Louisiana State, North Carolina, Pennsylvania, Notre Dame, Dartmouth, Yale, Amherst, Wesleyan and scores of other colleges. He devoted even more time to high schools.

Roy discouraged high soaring punts that could be run back by the safety man. "Always kick away from the receiver," he told his students. "Boot a low, scudding, thirty-five-yard kick that will hit the ground and roll another thirty-five yards, winding up out of bounds. What good is a Red Grange if he can't get his mitts on the ball?"

Mills was a wizard at kicking field goals. Nobody else had such control of a drop-kick. He used to stand on the corner of the goal line and curve the ball at right angles through the goal posts. Folks wouldn't believe it even when they saw it. One winter he stood on a basketball court and drop-kicked baskets from mid-floor. He was uncanny.

It was Mills who discovered Frank Carideo at Mt. Vernon High School and developed him into the most competent corner-kicker of his day. Knute Rockne didn't know anything about angle punting, but he had sense enough not to tamper with Carideo when the boy arrived at Notre Dame.

"Do it your way, kid," Rock said.

Mills always said that the three greatest drop-kickers of all time were Charley Brickley, Chicago's Walter Eckersall and Pat O'Dea of Wisconsin. Eckersall kicked five field goals against Illinois in 1905. Brickley did the same thing against Yale in 1913. Before the kick-off, Charley made my alma mater shiver with fear. What a demonstration of drop-kicking! He started on the ten-yard line and, retreating ten yards at a clip, he booted field goals all the way back to midfield. Then he turned in the opposite direction and repeated the stunt without a single miss.

They called Pat O'Dea The Human Kangaroo. He came from Australia and played for Wisconsin in the Nineties. Pat specialized in Rugby tricks. He would kick the ball on the dead run.

O'Dea caught a Minnesota punt at midfield in 1899, eluded Gil Dobie's flying tackle and, instead of running the ball, kicked it clear over the Gopher crossbar sixty yards away. The stunt broke the hearts of the Minnesota players, who were never in the ball game after that.

It was discussed earlier in this chapter how often Navy has defeated Army with field goals, but smiling Hank Garbisch gave the Middies some of their own medicine at Baltimore in 1924. The big guard, who wore a seraphic smile during the heat of action, had his toe count from long range that afternoon when the Pointers' ground attack bogged down against the stubborn Navy line.

The sentimental Dutchman had several good-luck charms concealed in the toe of his kicking shoe, including a letter from his mother. "Before each field goal attempt," Garbisch said, "I patted my toe and made a wish. I knew I couldn't miss."

He didn't miss, either. Four times he split the uprights!

Perhaps the two finest backfields ever seen in a service game between the Navy and the Army played in the 1926 production at Chicago's Soldiers Field, the only time the two Academies met west of the Atlantic Seaboard. Harry Wilson, Red Cagle, Chick Harding and John Murrell handled the ball for the Army that afternoon. The Navy matched this quartet man for man with Tom Hamilton, Allen Shapley, Hank Caldwell and Whitey Lloyd.

The first commandment in coaching is never underrate the enemy. Biff Jones of the Army ignored this. He started his second team. The Black Knights were two touchdowns behind before Jones could get the regulars warmed up.

Cagle scored from midfield on a typical weaving reverse to put the Army in front, but Shapley tied it up for Navy on a triple reverse that looked like something Pop Warner would spring.

The game was late getting started that afternoon, and night fell prematurely on Chicago's lake front. It was so dark in the last quarter that the players looked like wraiths flitting through the gloom. A million fireflies seemed to twinkle in the stands. They were glowing cigarettes held in trembling fingers. Nobody could tell whether Cagle had made good his final field-goal attempt —not even the officials.

After such a wild struggle, it seemed only fair to settle for a 21-21 tie.

15

The Mighty Mites

One answer to all the charges of recruiting, proselyting and subsidizing in college football you hear today is the little school—that with an enrollment running from 100 or so students up to 1,500. Did you know that for every large university in this country there are scores of small institutions which field football teams and take a lively interest in the game?

Little schools get few headlines, yet, far from the tumult of ticket hustlers, pool-sheet scrambling and well-paid publicists, they have an impressive impact on the game. There are, I guess, about 150 large schools with a total of about 5,200 football players which get most of the attention. But keep in mind that there are also 700 small colleges and junior colleges with more than 28,000 youths who play the game each autumn.

And where do these small-college athletes come from, do you suppose? From the coal mines or the cornfields or the road gang? Are they kidnapped off some other campus and carried under cover of night? Does it take a lot of urging to persuade them to follow the life of Whozes Tech? Are they chased and recruited—like the time Buck Bailey, of Washington State, ran Pest Welch, then assistant coach of Washington, into a ditch during a cross-country auto race after a 220-pound tackle prospect? Hardly.

Thousands of high school football players are wising up to percentages and flocking to schools like Western Maryland, Willamette, Colorado Mines, Haskell Institute and Western Reserve. I think the modern kid has become aware of the fact that out of seventy-five backfield candidates and thirty tackle aspirants at Mammoth U., eight or ten backs and four or five tackles are going to play virtually 100 per cent of the football.

"Boys," a Southern scout bluntly told a bunch of graduating high school seniors one time, "if we don't invite you, don't bother to come."

Harry Grayson tells the one about the time the Oklahoma president addressed the incoming freshman class. "Students," he announced, "we want a freshman class here that our football team will be proud of."

There's none of that stuff at the Pacific Lutheran Colleges of the country. Sure, the welcome mat is always out, but you come on your own accord. Fathers and high school coaches, digging the star dust out of their eyes, are realizing that plenty of action for a boy in a lesser league is preferable to four years as a goof or meathead on the Mammoth bench.

"There are two ways to get players," a small-college coach said. "Some little schools back up a bus to the big school's practice lot and load in the cast-offs when the squad cut comes. Or you can keep your eyes peeled for a particular type of prospect. The one I want is finishing high school a year ahead of his class and who, if he stayed another year, would become so hot in football that he'd be snapped up by one of the big schools. He's smart—he's just developing as a player—and usually he's available."

The small-college coach must constantly be alert for raids by big-time football's brash burglars. Otherwise, they'll grab every good halfback the little school has got. A few years ago a famous Texas school was caught sending telegrams to the ace of a tiny college eleven.

"What are you going to do?" the star was asked.

The young man deliberated. "I'll tell you," he finally said. "The way those fellows deal, if I ever have a boy of my own, I'm gonna darn well make sure he plays football at a small school, like his old man."

Professional team scouts, combing the back country for hidden talent, agree that the carefree rustic game is the most spectacular of all. "Big schools must play it close to the vest, always figuring percentages," one scout said. "You have to get out in the bush leagues where there's no pressure to see those what-the-heck triple reverses and lateral forwards."

Willamette University, a grid-conscious little Methodist school in Oregon, where they patch the pigskins and have never been known for dismissing a coach for losing, comes about as close as any school I know to the definition of a model small college, as given by the academicians: an institution with long tradition and history—usually dating to the Civil War—whose moderate endowment yields an income equal to one half its annual budget, and whose selected student body numbers in the neighborhood of 1,200 or so. The pioneer, Jason Lee, founded Willamette, one of the oldest universities in the West. One student applicant in every two fails to meet entrance requirements, a deliberate device to keep enrollment down and boneheads out.

Willamette has faced all the problems afflicting the little school which maintains a football team without benefit of ballyhoo, slush funds and other modern conveniences. For years, its Bearcats held title to the worst playing surface for football in eleven Western states.

A few years ago, a former Western Conference official who worked a Willamette game, told Al Stump, the magazine writer, that he was never so shocked in his life. "It was only drizzling," the official said, "but when I walked onto the field I immediately sank past my ankles in thick green mud. I've seen gooey fields, but this one was a hog wallow. You could smell it, too. I found out that the muck was 'ripe' because they hadn't bothered to scrape it off in three years."

The man from the big time was in for another surprise. After clearing the swamp of a mired-down dog and several splattered children, he prepared to blow his whistle. Just then the head linesman yelled: "If they kick it in the creek, I'll get the ball!"

"What creek?" asked the newcomer.

"The creek running alongside the field and through the grandstand," the linesman said. "It's a kind of millstream. Once they had to chase the ball a hundred yards downstream before they could get it out."

The official from the Midwest shuddered, blew his whistle, grabbed his nose tightly and sloshed bravely on down under the kick-off.

Small college coaches are jacks-of-all-jobs who generally serve as combined junior varsity and head coach, athletic director, equipment manager, purchasing agent, trainer, rubber, ticket manager, promotion man and employment bureau. They grow wistful when they read newspaper items telling how major college scouts travel 15,000 miles on scouting missions each season. Their own scouting mileage is usually zero, although they yearn each autumn to get an advance look at their conference opponents. Spying takes time and money. The small college has neither to spare.

The small school's chief headache is financial. Football is usually a losing proposition. Rising costs have caused not a few of the smaller schools to quit the sport since World War II. In 1941, however, Willamette made one of its rare grabs for bigger stakes, and has never ceased to regret it. When the Honolulu Shriners guaranteed the little Oregon school $5,500 for two games in the Islands, the university reversed its policy on long trips and accepted. It was a pleasant outing for the team, even after losing the opener to the University of Hawaii. On Saturday, December sixth, the Bearcats bought post cards and trinkets in the Kalakaua Avenue souvenir shops and turned in early, preparatory to a morning workout.

Before noon the next morning they were feverishly digging trenches and stringing barbed wire for the Army on Waikiki Beach. Those waterspouts they'd seen offshore at breakfast hadn't been target practice bombs after all.

"Wow!" cried one player. "I never thought they'd call off the game on account of war!" Willamette since has had an aversion to intersectional games that will take years to wear off.

Everything considered, bush football has remarkably few apologies to make. It has been the backbone of the game since a small college—Rutgers—started the whole thing against Princeton on November 6, 1869. Rutgers won that first game of intercollegiate football, 6-4. In 1905, it was a photo of a bloody-faced Swarthmore, Pennsylvania, lineman which caused my old friend, Teddy Roosevelt, almost to blow the roof off the White House. Little Swarthmore's man had been hammered to pulp by the behemoths of Penn. The President was incensed at such carnage and demanded a rules shake-up to get away from massive charging formations. The result, in 1906, was legalization of the forward pass—today the game's most exciting weapon.

I wonder what would have happened to the forward pass if the Harvard Stadium had never been built. When the crusade against injuries swept the country after that Swarthmore incident, Walter Camp decided to modify the rules to resemble English Rugby. This called for widening the playing field so as to make laterals more effective. Camp bumped into a snag right there—the immovable Harvard Stadium.

This huge concrete structure, built in 1903, was designed to hug the boundary of the field as tightly as a woman's skirt. The Harvard crowd had obviously sunk too much cash into the stadium to permit the field to be widened. Camp had no alternative. He had to forget his Rugby ideas in favor of the forward pass.

Who threw the first pass? I have heard a number of versions, but most old-timers credit little Wesleyan, of Connecticut, against Yale.

Though he used the pass as a strategic weapon, Rockne never went haywire about throwing the ball as some of the air-minded modern teams have gone. L. H. Gregory, veteran sports editor of the *Portland Oregonian* and one of the slickest grid observers in the country, gives you a new twist on the dangers of too much aerial emphasis:

"A baseball pitcher wouldn't think of throwing hard before warming up," said Gregory, "yet a quarterback in football often will be heaving a ball quite hard in pre-game passing practice with only slight preliminary loosening up.

"In the early part of the 1952 professional football season, both Norm Van Brocklin and Bob Waterfield, the Los Angeles Rams' quarterbacks, had sore arms from too much practice passing in fall camp, unavoidable because the club had no other quarterback candidates to take part of the load. Since then the Rams, as well as other football clubs, try to have at least three and sometimes four quarterbacks in their camps."

As a coach incubator, the minors have kept the big time well supplied. Dana Bible, Gus Dorais, Fielding Yost, Ossie Solem, Matty Bell, Tuss McLaughry, Clipper Smith, Bo McMillin, Greasy Neale, Carl Snavely, and dozens of others started in the outlands.

You could pick a nifty All-America from among the small schools. The professionals will tell you that no greater end ever played in the National Football League than Cal Hubbard, the big guy from tiny Geneva College who graduated to the major leagues as an umpire. Few quarterbacks could match Benny Boynton, the Purple Streak from Williams College in the Berkshires. And stunners, such as Arnie Herber, Regis College, and Bulldog Turner, Hardin-Simmons, are constantly popping up. West Coast addicts don't think they will ever again see the likes of little Pacific Lutheran College's Marvelous Marvs—Marv Harshman and Marv Tommervik.

My good friend Whitney Martin, the widely read Associated Press sports columnist and a mighty keen observer of the football scene for many years, agrees with my opinion that the quality of the players is more important than the size of the squad in the building of a solid football team.

"I recall that around 1912 Lawrence College of Appleton, Wisconsin, had a squad that numbered only eighteen or twenty players at the most," Whitney told me. "The team was coached by Mark Catlin, famous Chicago University player under Coach Stagg. The players were rugged lads, and it was nothing for the eleven starting players to play an entire game. Catlin even had the ends and backs play without padding so they would be faster. That really toughened them up.

"The team at that time played Wisconsin each fall, and gave the Badgers all they were looking for. I know it lost once by only one touchdown, and I'm not sure but it tied the Big Ten team once.

"I, myself, played at Coe College in Cedar Rapids, Iowa, under Coach Moray Eby, a fine tutor. It is a comparatively small school with the squad, at least at that time, quite limited.

"We went out to Ames and defeated Iowa State, 6-0, about 1920 and played the entire game without a substitution. And Iowa State had a big squad of big men.

"The small college teams, if well coached, often play a first-class brand of football. Their games aren't accompanied by the whoopla of the big games in the big stadiums, but they are a very real part of the American football scene. Football is everybody's game. Without the hundreds of smaller colleges participating, interest would fade gradually, as interest in major-league baseball would fade without minor league and sandlot ball."

Centre College, under Coach Charley Moran in the early twenties, even crashed the big-time momentarily. Uncle Charley was one of those all-around fellows who doubled in brass as coach, trainer, equipment man and father confessor to his players. He was also a talent scout extraordinary, and on vacation imported a tough-fibered band of Texans to represent the Golden White. One of 'em was Bo McMillin.

Uncle Charley was also a clever publicity man. He pinned the name "Praying Colonels" upon his Kentucky pupils and was mighty happy when Grantland Rice widely circulated the nickname.

"My players hold a prayer meeting before each game," he let it be known.

One day the Centre College team was checking into the Vanderbilt Hotel in New York when Uncle Charley happened to see Grantland Rice entering the lobby. Moran snapped his men to attention.

"Down on your knees quick, you so-and-so's," he muttered, "here comes Grantland Rice!"

Little Centre made headlines in 1921 by upending Harvard, 6-0. On their trip to Cambridge, the Southerners were lavishly entertained by the Crimson reception committee. All this partying disturbed Uncle Charley. He feared his men might lose their fighting edge. He called the players aside in the locker room just before the game.

"Listen," he said. "I know you guys have been nicely entertained by these Harvard chaps, but just remember one thing when you go onto the field this afternoon.

"Everyone of those bums votes the straight Republican ticket!"

16

Sizing Up the More Moderns

Yale beat Princeton, 19-0, in my last college game, and as I walked off the field, a friend grabbed me by the arm and asked, "Heff, ol' boy, how does it feel to be through with football forever?"

If I had had John Paul Jones' knack for epigrams I might have answered: "Me quit football? Why, I've only begun to play!"

That would have been the truth then. But as I sit in the stands and wait for the opening whistle these Saturday afternoons, I wish it were still the truth.

Maybe I can't get out there in a uniform anymore, but I still have a few definite ideas about the way the modern generation plays football. For one thing, I notice they go in for big, heavy lines today. Strength alone won't enable a kid to handle brawny attackers. They've got to be taught the proper stance. My stance was the secret of my ability to get position on kids bigger than I ever was. I stood up to it! Yes, sir, both on attack and defense I stood more or less erect, knees bent in a slight crouch, body leaning forward from the hips, legs spread about three feet apart, left foot advanced when playing left guard. I hit my man with a shoulder lunge on attack and used my hands to start his head in the direction I wanted to move him, when we were on defense. A man's body must go where his head goes. Oh, yes, I know the semi-erect stance is considered football heresy today. Kids are now told to get down on one or both knees, with their hands on the ground. They won't let a boy stand up to it any more.

I said it earlier in this book and I will say it again—a man is no good on his knees! Nobody would have heard of Heffelfinger if Walter Camp had made me take it kneeling down. Our Yale linemen had their heads up where they could see what was happening across the neutral zone. We never went down unless we had to. We whipped underneath our foes from that half crouch something like the way a hammer thrower pivots his body in the release.

"It can't be done!" modern coaches retort. "They'd put you flat on your back!"

Nuts! I did it for almost fifty years against first-class opposition, and nobody ever put me on my back.

"Well, you were a physical freak," I can hear the skeptics saying. Wrong again. It was method, not muscle, that gave me the jump on linemen of my day. Listen, it wasn't so many years ago that I could still prove that statement on the field against young huskies. Now you'll have to take my word for it.

When you're up on your feet you're in position to get into enemy territory like a thief running from the cops. You can't do that so quickly if you're down on the prayer rug. From a semi-standing stance you can look the defense formation over, or size up the enemy grouping attack. By watching the ball closely, you can detect the slightest flexing of the enemy center's hands—the tip-off that he's going to snap it—and thus time your charge with the ball.

Our old Yale line always charged the ball. Few modern lines do. They watch their opponents instead of the ball. They don't get the jump. Pa Corbin's linemen were strong and fast rather than big and ponderous. I could run the hundred in good time. In my senior year I stripped at about 190, give or take a pound, and stood 6-foot-2, but most of my mates weighed thirty pounds less.

Bert Metzger demonstrated that a guard doesn't have to be big to shine as an interferer. The Notre Dame star of olden days couldn't have scaled more than 165 pounds in his mud-caked football gear. He was a stubby, thick-set chap who never failed to get a blocking angle.

When Bert first reported for football at Notre Dame, he was lost in the shuffle of giant candidates. Rockne spotted him one day and asked:

"Son, what position do you play?"

"I'm a guard," said Metzger chestily.

"Aren't you rather little for a guard?" Rockne demanded.

"Maybe," Bert admitted, "but I'm a little bit tough!"

Metzger was all of that, as Rockne quickly discovered. Bert had a habit of pulling out too soon, and used to bump into Marty Brill. Rockne was annoyed.

"What's dumber than a dumb Dutchman?" he exploded.

"A smart Swede!" retorted Metzger. At least that's the story Rock told me.

What happens to a boxer who bores in blindly with

his head down? He gets his ears knocked off! He can't ward off blows which he doesn't see coming. Well, the same thing goes for a football lineman. I never kept my head down. I wanted to see what was coming, and be up on my feet where I could deliver.

If you're up against a much better man, then you can fall down and grab legs; but stay on your feet as long as you can. They tell me I'd be mousetrapped if I charged fast today with my legs driving. Boloney! I'd have my eyes open and fight off the mousetrapper before he got me. I never made a blind charge. I drove in toward the pressure point and mussed things up before the interference could form.

If you hit 'em first you catch 'em off balance.

Another thing that makes me laugh about football today is the modern fans' aversion to Saturday afternoon slaughters. Remember what I said about Yale's celebrated team of '88, the one that won thirteen, lost none and tied none and ran up 698 points to zero? People weren't so sensitive to blood and broken bones in those days. They loved it. Today, if a baseball team goes crazy and hits a lot of home runs and leads, 13-2, the fans all get up and go home by the seventh inning. I remember one year when Army ran up fifty-four points on Harvard. When Red Blaik, a fine coach, ran in his first team, most of the audience got up and left in disgust. You'll stay to the last put-out in a ball game with the score, 1-0. Nobody will leave a football field until the final whistle if the score is 7-6 or 13-6. Things change—let's face it.

Over the hubbub and confusion and contention regarding the state of college football today, the All-America business goes on. It occurs to me that it has grown too big for its britches. I was on the first All-America team in history. This was back in 1889, the year the hysteria originated in the otherwise perfectly normal mind of Caspar Whitney. It was in actuality an all-star Big Three team. Only Yale, Harvard and Princeton were represented. In those days, as I have said, the Big Three was about all there was to American football.

You may be interested in knowing who was on that team. Cumnock, of Harvard, and Stagg, of Yale, were the ends; Cowan, of Princeton, and Gill, of Yale, the tackles; Cranston, of Harvard, and myself, the guards. George, of Princeton, the center; Edgar Allen Poe, of Princeton, the quarterback; Lee, of Harvard, and Channing, of Princeton, the halfbacks, and Snake Ames, of Princeton, the fullback.

In my day there was some sense and logic in the All-America selections, because there weren't many good teams, and naturally there weren't many good players. It wasn't hard for Walter Camp to pick out the eleven best. But today the All-America is a joke. There are hundreds of excellent players, and trying to rate one above the other is an impossible job.

Here I am, a man who had been named on the very first All-America ever picked, and I am putting a blast on the idea. This, you must be saying, is nothing short of treason. Call it what you will. I think it's pure nonsense, and furthermore, I don't think anybody pays any attention to the All-America picks of today. Any schoolboy must realize the absurdity of the thing. I have seen as many as a dozen teams play in a season, and I wouldn't attempt to name the eleven best players I saw. It would be much easier for me to name twenty or thirty, and then I wouldn't be sure I was right.

Joe Williams, for years one of my favorite sports columnists, once asked me, "Pudge, what do you think of the modern game?"

"What do you mean the modern game?" I snorted. "In some form or another we did about everything that is done in football today. Of course, we didn't forward pass because it was against the rules. We had laterals, but they weren't used much. Our system of defense and offense was fundamentally the same as it is today. Except for refinements and a closer attention to details, due to larger coaching staffs, it's basically the same game. And all this talk about systems is largely twaddle."

Along these same lines, somebody once said something about mousetrapping to Pop Warner, and Pop said, "That's a new name for it. But call it a mousetrapping play or a sucker play, I don't think a lineman who knows his business has much to fear from it."

A number of seasons ago, Iowa had terrific success using only fifteen or sixteen players to a game, which confirmed a pet theory of mine. I have always maintained that modern coaches use too many men. Football is essentially a team game, and how in the name of Billy Blazes can you develop unity of performance by using thirty or forty players to a game. With the platoon system abolished, it is my notion that a coach will get better results if he will pick a starting line-up at the beginning of the season and stick to it. The coach will have fifteen or sixteen fine players instead of thirty or forty semi-ordinary ones.

Of course, it has always been highly ridiculous to me that a young man can't play sixty minutes of football without fatigue. That's why I was happy when they got rid of platoon football. It separated the men from the boys.

Joe Sheehan, who has been covering football for *The New York Times* for the last twenty years, told me that he thought the 1953 substitution rules change was the best thing to happen to football in years. "Two-platoon football had developed specialization to a ridiculous extreme," said the president of the New York Football Writers Association. "Now once again, the 'whole' football player is in there."

Why, even the players came up with perfect rebuttals.

"If you're in shape," said Johnny Lujack, the old Notre Dame star, "you play both ways without getting tired. The backs have little to do on most defensive plays, so get a rest when the other side has the ball. Offensively, linemen often don't do much more than lunge at opponents, particularly when the play is going to the opposite side. So they rest when you have the ball."

Stalwarts like Bill Stits of UCLA, Bruce Bosley of West Virginia and Don Miller of Southern Methodist liked the switch back to the old game because it was now every man for himself all the way down the line. They stressed the fact that the athlete who is in good condition is freer from injuries.

Remember what I said about teamwork? It makes me happy when I hear young fellows like Johnny Melear, Miami University's quarterback in 1953, testify: "The limited substitution rule restored teamwork. It gave us more unity during the season. In the two-platoon system, it was hard to get the feeling of genuine teamwork because the units were so completely separate during practice."

A couple of years ago a star New England high school halfback was snapped up by a southern college. His old coach heard nothing of the lad as a sophomore, and when he returned home for the holidays asked him why.

"I made the mistake of making some tackles," the boy explained, "but it won't happen again. You'll hear of me next fall, when I'll be on the offensive team."

The coach did.

The young man, you see, just quit making tackles. And that, sir, is what the platoons had brought college football to.

You heard grumbling in some quarters when the platoon system was banished, but Brig. Gen. Bob Neyland was positive that the fans were in favor of the Old Deal. The former Tennessee coach was on the committee that abolished swing-shift football.

"On the day before we went into our meeting, the waitress at breakfast, knowing we were on the rules committee, said she hoped we did something about the two-platoon system," the General related. "I was riding in a taxicab, and the driver remarked that he hoped we would abolish the two-platoon. The hostess at the hotel said she hoped we did something about the two-platoon. Some coaches may have objected, but I certainly knew how the fans felt."

Whitney Martin also sees football as a game for all-around players, and not just specialists.

"I think," he said, "it was a good thing for the game when the so-called two-platoon football was eliminated.

It was a relief in 1953 to see the ball change hands without a score of players rushing on and off the field. Now you can keep track of them, and a player is in the game long enough for you to see whether he can tackle and defend against passes as well as run with the ball and kick or pass.

"I think that the boys get more satisfaction out of knowing they are capable of playing all-around football, instead of playing on just offense or defense. It is a fine game now, and I hope they don't tamper with the rules too much. The development of the forward and lateral pass has added greatly to the spectator's enjoyment, and has made ball handling into an art.

"Basically, there's not much new in the game. If you will check back you'll find that great coaches such as Stagg, Warner, Rockne and Dobie tried nearly everything that you see today, at least as far as the rules permitted at the time.

"There's still no substitute for good blocking and good tackling and good running, and an athlete who can do those things well could play the game in any era."

Now I've got to get in my annual squawk about the equipment the modern boys wear. I have never been able to understand it. They wear too much. In most cases it's just added weight to lug, and it doesn't necessarily prevent cuts and bruises. Ask any old-timer. He will tell you the same thing. My old friend, Greasy Neale, will tell you.

"I do agree on this equipment thing," he told me. "If I was playing out there I wouldn't want one of those shoulder guards, but just some felt to give me a little protection and that's all."

184

You see, we simply let our hair grow long in our day and slipped it through a turtleneck sweater.

Don't tell anyone, but I was the first football player ever to wear shinguards. When Pa Corbin saw them strapped to my shins, he yowled, "Softie! You can wear those sissy things if you want to, but as long as I'm captain here you'll have to wear them inside your socks. I don't want any teammate of mine showing a weakness like that!" I threw the dang things away.

I'm not one of those sentimental old fogeys who lives in the past. I like the speed of the modern game, and I wish there was a way of getting, say, our Yales of '88 on the same field with a team the strength of Biggie Munn's recent Michigan State powerhouses. I'm not saying we'd win, but it would be a heck of a battle.

Yes, boiled down to its essentials, football is a great game. And look how it has grown. College games on Friday nights and Saturday afternoons and the professionals all over the country on Sunday. This television is amazing. Come to think of it, I was playing football before there were automobiles, wirefotos, newsreels, or aerial views from helicopters.

I would love to live another eighty-six years—just to see what's around the corner!

Football, anyone?

A Final Tribute

By Joe Williams

It got so in the later years that even some of the Old Blues around the Yale Club in New York made gentle mockeries at the expense of Pudge Heffelfinger and his militant dedication to red meat football as he liked to call it. But that was one of the things I liked best about him, the stanch manner in which he stood up for his beliefs, the unyielding support he gave his principles.

To Pudge football was something of a religion. He had got so much out of the game as an undergraduate that it just logically had to mean more to him than most of his contemporaries. Perhaps this was why he put such a high value on it. It was as if he had probed deeper and got closer to its real meaning.

I often heard him say: "A game that can keep you young and vibrant and all steamed up is a precious thing."

Because of the oft told story about the charity game he played in when he was in his fifties and because he was such a big man (and from Minnesota, too) the casual reader might understandingly have pictured him as a Paul Bunyan with a varsity Y. Actually Pudge was more a brain man than a muscle man, and football must always remember him for his revolutionary concepts of line play, a much more revealing and significant measure of

185

the man than the simple physical culture fact that he had the good sense to keep his body in shape long after his college days were over.

I always tried to make a point to have Pudge as one of our honored guests at the Scripps-Howard Coach of the Year Dinner. I have a delightful memory of the year we saluted Charley Caldwell of Princeton in Dallas, Texas. Pudge sat with Amos Alonzo Stagg, another enduring and imposing Yale landmark. They had been classmates under The Elms and played varsity football together.

I sensed the evening hadn't been a complete social success for my old friend, and, somewhat abased, he presently admitted this was so.

"You know how much I think of Lonnie Stagg," he said. "One of the finest men God ever put breath in. And I guess the finest coach football ever had. But there are times when he goes too far."

It turned out that Stagg was enthusiastic about the subtle brush block as it is practiced in the T defense. Had it been anybody else but the intensely serious Stagg there would have been reason to suspect a gag. In any case, nothing could have been devised that would have distressed Old Iron Sides more.

Nevertheless, Pudge, as you noted in this engaging book, could scarcely have been labeled a professional old-timer, and certainly he was not a biased traditionalist. A large part of football history was written by the Big Three. Yet Pudge thought it beyond argument the best football today was played in the Big Ten.

Although he was named at guard on every all-time All-America team ever selected, he came to regard such selections as sheer nonsense. And while he went back to the Poes, Coys, Thorpes, Brickleys et al., the best back-field he ever saw was that of the 1946 Army team which spotlighted Doc Blanchard and Glenn Davis.

As a matter of fact, Pudge was tenaciously old-fash-ioned about only one proposition, namely, that line play was not exactly an ideal calling for the Christine Jorgen-sens.

Index

The italic figures in parentheses tell in what section a picture of the person is located. For example, there is a picture of Frankie Albert in the photo section following page 64.

189

190

192